Success at Bible Teaching

Sam Binkley, Jr.
Martin M. Broadwell

Gospel Armory
PUBLISHING

Published by:
Gospel Armory Publishing
Bowling Green, Kentucky
www.GospelArmory.com

Reformatting by MilePost Publications

Special thanks to Sam Binkley, Jr. and to Marty Broadwell (on behalf of his father) for permission to republish this material.

Printed in the United States of America

ISBN: 978-1-942036-09-8

TABLE OF CONTENTS

To all who teach the word of God, especially to my mother who taught me in my youth and my wife who taught our children and who encourages me in my efforts to teach.
Sam Binkley

To all the Bible teachers – including my mother – who made me so fond of the Bible as the perfect guide to life and life after death.
Martin M. Broadwell

PREFACE

While in the absolute sense teaching is to give instruction, it cannot be said that the purpose for teaching has been accomplished until a change has taken place in the person(s) taught. Imparting the information to the student(s) is the means necessary to bringing about the change, but the change effected in the lives of those who are taught is the result of the teaching done. It is not difficult to understand this as it relates to teaching one how to operate a piece of machinery, conduct a chemical analysis, or a scientific experiment. The same principle applies in teaching the word of God.

The purpose of teaching people the Bible is that they may undergo a change (be converted) and become children of God (new creatures in Christ Jesus). Jesus gave the great commission to His apostles to "go teach all nations" (Matt. 28:19)[1] in order that the believers might be baptized into Christ and thereby become "new creatures" (2 Cor. 5:17). The new birth, the process by which one becomes a child of God, involves teaching. This birth is "of water and the Spirit" (John 3:5), and the part the Spirit has in bringing about the new birth is accomplished by the gospel. The Bible teaches that we are born again of the incorruptible seed, the word of God, which by the gospel is preached unto you (1 Peter 1:23-25). The begetting, a necessary part of the new birth, is done by the

---

[1] All Scriptures quoted in this volume are from the King James Version unless otherwise noted.

gospel which is the word of truth (see also 1 Cor. 4:15; James 1:18).

In bringing about the change in one's life that God requires, one cannot overlook the necessity of teaching the right thing, the word of God. It is the Scripture inspired of God that is able to make the man of God perfect, or complete (2 Tim. 3:16, 17). For this reason we must teach only the word of God (2 Tim. 4:2; 2 John 9-11).

The Bible is also clear in pointing out that the Lord expects us to develop skill in teaching His word to others so that they may know how to become new creatures in Christ and also be shown the advantages of becoming such. As Christians we are to be ready always to give an answer to every man who asks us a reason for the hope that is in us (1 Peter 3:15), and to let our speech be with grace, seasoned with salt, that we may know *how* we ought to answer every man (Col. 4:6). These Scriptures indicate that we must not only know what to say in our teaching, but also *how* we say it.

A familiar Scripture showing us the importance of study (2 Tim. 2:15) also shows the importance of using or handling the word of God properly. The New American Standard Version renders the passage "Be diligent to present yourself approved to God as a workman who does not need to be ashamed, handling accurately the word of truth." This indicates that some skill is required in the use we make of the word of truth. Elders in the Lord's church are specifically told to be "apt to teach" (1 Tim. 3:2). To Titus Paul wrote that elders are to be able to use the faithful word to exhort and convince the gainsayers (Titus 1:9).

These are but a few of the Scriptures which tell us something of what teaching is all about. It is the hope of the authors that this volume will be of some help to all Bible teachers in causing the greatest possible number of people to "receive with meekness the engrafted word, which is able to save your souls" (James 1:21).

PROLOGUE

We congratulate you on your interest in improving your teaching skill. Hopefully, this book will enable you to do just that, when used along with meaningful practice. But we feel we should remind you that students don't learn theoretically, so teaching texts aren't going to do much good if they contain only theory. We have tried to give the Bible teacher something that goes beyond theory – some practical examples. There are no great, profound findings in this volume. Much of what you read you will either already know, or could have figured out with a little thought. So we attempt these two things :

1. To remind you of things you know but may have forgotten to use, and
2. To give you some reasons for the things you are already doing but may have wondered if they were the right things to do.

With this much said, we urge you to devote yourself diligently to improving yourself as a Bible teacher. There is no other more important task assigned to us!

Sam Binkley, Jr.
Martin M. Broadwell

PART I

THE BIBLE TEACHER

CHAPTERS 1-5

CHAPTER 1

THE CHRISTIAN AS A TEACHER

Acts 8:4
Therefore they that were scattered abroad went every where preaching the word.

Introduction

There are many aspects to the life of the Christian. The Christian, in his relation to God and his fellowman, should consider such things as his holiness of character, his worship of God, his attitude toward his brethren and also to the people of the world. He should also consider himself as a teacher of the word of God.

Teaching has always had an important place in God's plan. God chose Abram because He knew he was a man who would command his household (Gen. 18:19). During the Mosaic period He instructed parents to teach their children diligently (Deut. 6:4-9). Ezra was a man who had his heart set to study the law of the Lord, to practice it, and to teach it to others (Ezra 7:10). God's requirements for His people in the New Testament are no different in this respect. Jesus clearly stated that one must be taught of God in order to come to Him (John 6:44-45), and when He gave the great commission to the apostles He said they were to teach, baptize, and then teach the baptized (Matt. 28:19-20). Not only must one be taught in order to become a child of God, but teaching is necessary also to growing in the grace and knowledge of the Lord (1 Pet. 2:1-2; Heb. 5:12-14). With the emphasis that the Bible places upon teaching, every Christian should want to be a teacher and should want to be the best teacher possible.

He Is Expected To Teach

When Jesus told his disciples to go teach all nations and to baptize those that were taught He also said for them to teach the baptized to observe all things He had commanded them (Matt. 28:19-20). It is quite evident from this that disciples of Christ are not only learners of Christ, but are also teachers of the words of Christ. Paul's statement to Timothy, "And the things that thou hast heard of me among many witnesses, the same commit thou to faithful men, who shall be able to teach others also" (2 Tim. 2:2), shows that Christians are expected to be teachers of the will of Christ. The early disciples understood they were expected to teach, for when they were scattered by the persecution that arose against the church which was at Jerusalem they went everywhere preaching the word (Acts 8:1-4).

He Should Want To Teach

One cannot become a disciple of the Lord until he has first been taught of God (John 6:44-45; Heb. 8:11). This should cause those who have already become Christians to want to teach others what they themselves have learned that they may share in the blessings of being in Christ. The Christian should want to be a teacher, even though he may realize that he will receive heavier judgment (James 3:1), because of the good he may do in saving himself and others.

Jesus not only showed His love for man by giving Himself as a sacrifice to God (Eph. 5:2), but also by teaching man how to be righteous in the sight of God. The Father was with Christ while He lived among men because He always did those things that were pleasing to God (John 8:29), and we are promised that we will receive the things we ask of Him when we keep His commandments and do the things that are pleasing in His sight (1 John 3:22). Doing the things that please God includes teaching others the way of salvation. Christians should want to become teachers because in doing so they are instrumental in saving the most valuable thing in the world, the soul of man (Matt. 16:26), and are at the same time becoming more like the Christ whom they serve.

He Should Want To Be A Better Teacher

The Bible emphasizes the importance of Christians engaging in the act of teaching. The Bible likewise shows the necessity of teaching the right doctrine (Gal. 1:8-9; 2 John 9-11; Rev. 22:18-19). As we remind ourselves of the importance of teaching and of teaching the right doctrine let us not lose sight of the importance of developing and using skill in our teaching. In 1 Tim. 3:2 and 2 Tim. 2:24 the expression "apt to teach" is translated from a word in the Greek, *DIDAKTIKOS*, which means to be skilled in teaching. Therefore not only must an elder be apt to teach, but also the servant of God.

The New Testament scriptures teach that some (newborn babes in Christ) need the milk of the word (1 Pet. 2:1-2), whereas others who have experienced more spiritual growth (Heb. 5:12-14) need the stronger meat of the word. Determining who needs the milk and who needs the meat in their spiritual diet and presenting it in an appealing manner requires some skill. The apostle Paul showed this when he said, "Let your speech be alway with grace, seasoned with salt, that ye may know how ye ought to answer every man" (Col. 4:6). And again, "I have fed you with milk, and not with meat: for hitherto ye were not able to bear it, neither yet now are ye able" (1 Cor. 3:2). He went on to point out that the reason they still were not able to bear the meat was that they were yet carnal. Seeing the value the Lord places upon exercising skill in our teaching, we should be as concerned about developing and improving our ability to teach as we are about any other phase of our spiritual growth and development. If we ever expect to be perfect or complete – and this state we can attain by the proper use of the scriptures (2 Tim. 3:16-17) – we must develop our skill as teachers, for so much of what the Lord expects of us as laborers in His vineyard involves the teaching of His word.

DISCUSSION ACTIVITIES

1. Let each person in the group think of how he really came to know of God. (Some will have learned of God through their own study; most will have been taught by someone.) Let each think of what it was about the person that taught him that convinced him that God was real and that the Bible was the answer to reaching God... to knowing about Him.

2. Compare the warning "Be not many of you teachers" (ASV, James 3:1) with the exhortation to Timothy

to teach the things that he had received to faithful men "who shall be able to teach others also" (ASV, 2 Tim. 2:2). Make this comparison by having one half of the group discuss points in favor of the warning and the other half discuss the points in favor of the exhortation. Have each present their arguments, then come to a conclusion in light of the other scriptures given in this chapter.

3. If teaching is a skill – and we say it is a number of times in this book – how can I be a good teacher if I've never taught?

4. 2 Tim. 2:24 speaks of one being apt to teach to be a servant (as we pointed out, literally, "skilled in teaching"). What about someone who says that teachers are born, not made-then goes on to say that "I don't have it, so I'll just let those who are born with it do the teaching"?

5. Discuss what might have happened if Priscilla and Aquila had decided that it wasn't their responsibility to teach Apollos. What evidence do we have that Apollos already had done damage with his incomplete doctrine (Acts 19:1-5)?

Deut. 6:4-9

Hear, O Israel: The Lord our God is one Lord: And thou shalt love the Lord thy God with all thine heart, and with all thy soul, and with all thy might. And these words, which I command thee this day, shall be in thine heart: And thou shalt teach them diligently unto thy children, and shalt talk of them when thou sittest in thine house, and when thou walkest by the way, and when thou liest down, and when thou risest up, And thou shalt bind them for a sign upon thine hand, and they shall be as frontlets between thine eyes. And thou shalt write them upon the posts of thy house, and on thy gates.

CHAPTER 2

THE BIBLE AS A TEACHER-TRAINING MANUAL

Acts 8:35
Then Philip opened his mouth, and began at the same scripture, and preached unto him Jesus.

The Message Is Inspired

The Bible is the best place to go to learn how to be a successful teacher of the word of God. There is no better place to learn what to teach or how best to teach it. God gave us His word that we might know how to serve Him acceptably while here on earth. The Bible claims to be "inspired of God" (2 Tim. 3:16). The next verse says that the scriptures inspired of God are able to make the man of God perfect, furnishing him completely unto every good work. It should be observed that the word "inspired" is from a word in the Greek language which literally means "God-breathed" and the word "perfect" means complete or mature. In the previous chapter we have shown that one thing God wants His people to be is teachers. Therefore we conclude the Bible is able to make us the kind of teachers God wants us to be.

Other passages which show the Bible did not originate with man, but came from God, would include the one which says that it was according to His divine power that He gave "unto us all things that pertain unto life and godliness" (2 Pet. 1:3). Paul also wrote that we should not "think of men above that which is written" (1 Cor. 4:6). A passage that should be studied carefully on this point is 1 Cor. 2:1-13 in which the apostle showed that things he taught were revealed unto him by the Holy Spirit that our faith might not "stand in the wisdom of men, but in the power of God" (v. 5) and that the Holy Spirit chose the words, hence guiding the writer, "combining spiritual things with spiritual words" (v. 13, ASV). Truly the Bible is a teacher-training manual, but more than that it is God's inspired textbook on the subject.

The Teachers Were Often Guided By The Holy Spirit

Jesus promised the apostles that He would send the Holy Spirit to guide them into all truth (John 16:13). Jesus also promised them that the Holy Spirit would teach them all things, bring to their remembrance what He had taught them, testify of Him, and show them things to come (John 14:26; 15:26; 16:13). After His resurrection, when Jesus gave them the commission to go into all the world and preach the gospel to every creature, He also told them to tarry in Jerusalem until they were "endued with power from on high" before they began their work of teaching (Luke 24:49).

That Peter and the other apostles were thus guided by the Holy Spirit in the beginning of their work of preaching is evident from Acts 2:1-4. Study the sermon recorded in this chapter and observe not only the message itself, but the manner of presentation. Of course we are not trying to minimize the importance of the message, but are simply calling attention to the fact that we can learn something of the *how* of teaching as well as the *what* by studying the Bible. Surely the Lord approved of the way they taught as well as what they taught, and just that surely we can learn something of how we can effectively teach the word of the Lord today. Of course we realize that Peter, being guided by the Holy Spirit as he was, could know things about their needs that we are not able to know in teaching situations today, but observe that it was in reply to a question which they asked that Peter told them what to do to have their sins forgiven (Acts 2:36-38).

One of the lessons we can learn from this approved example is the value of knowing the needs of those whom we seek to teach. One good way to learn this is to give them an opportunity to tell you. In teaching techniques this is sometimes called "feedback." The teacher needs to receive information back from the pupil that he may know how far advanced the pupil is and how to proceed in order to bring him along further in the learning process.

Wise Men Were Teaching

Even if we can't prove that the prophets and apostles were inspired in their teaching *methods*, at least we know that they were wise men and had gifts of wisdom and knowledge. It stands to reason that God would have been careful in giving His message to people who were going to have the responsibility to teach others. It's unlikely that He would have wanted someone trusted with His message who would do a very poor job of teaching, especially since the population was without any other source of knowledge – the Bible not yet available to them.

Jesus Was A Teacher Teacher

Jesus spent approximately 3-1/2 years with His disciples during which time He was preparing them for the work He had for them to do in the establishment and growth of His kingdom. This work was primarily that of teaching His word. Jesus, therefore, taught them to teach.

Jesus used various methods in the teaching that He did. One of the methods was that of answering a question with a question (Matt. 21:23-27). This got the student involved immediately and gave Jesus the opportunity to emphasize the thing he needed the most. By using this method today we can also learn what the student is thinking and what points he needs. Jesus also used the method of contrast. In the sermon on the mount (Matt. 5:21-48), He repeatedly showed the difference between what they had heard "by them of old time" (v. 21) and what He said unto them.

The fact that Jesus, after His resurrection and before his ascension (Matt. 28:19), commanded His disciples to "go teach all nations" is an indication that He taught them to teach. When some in the church today begin to make excuses that they do not have the background to become teachers they should look in the New Testament at the background of the apostles and note that they became teachers. Teaching others the things we have learned is one way disciples of Christ help in the saving of souls and also become like Christ, whose likeness we are in and in whose footsteps we should seek to follow.

Examples Of Techniques

Jesus used different techniques in His teaching. We have already mentioned in this chapter that He answered a question with a question (Matt. 21:23-27). He used this technique on other occasions also. Experiences have demonstrated that this procedure gets people involved in the learning process in a way that enables them to discover truth for themselves. It is certainly much easier to accept something which we discover for ourselves than that which we are told by someone else.

Not only did Jesus use the method of contrast in the sermon on the mount, but this is also essentially what Paul did in his discourse on Mars' hill (Acts 17). He pointed out that they had gods of their own making which they served, and in contrast to that there was the God they worshipped in ignorance whom he declared unto them (Acts 17:23).

The process of going from the known to the unknown, which is a basic principle in the learning process, was used by different men in the New Testament in their teaching. One of the clear examples where this technique was employed was in Philip teaching the eunuch (Acts 8). When Philip approached the chariot and heard the eunuch reading he asked him if he understood what he was reading. The eunuch knew that the language of the prophet which he was reading described the death of someone, but he did not know whether it was the prophet himself or some other man (v. 34). Philip proceeded from this scripture and "preached unto him Jesus" (v. 35). There is obviously some overlapping in the techniques that were used. In the example we just noticed we can see the use of the technique we now want to look at in more detail.

Determining the point at which a student has progressed and starting there is a very important thing to remember in teaching, especially in spiritual matters. The story is told that a preacher (I believe it was T. B. Larimore), while talking with a man about his soul, repeatedly said, "The Bible teaches us to do this," and would then give the chapter and verse for the point. After he had continued this for some time the man then spoke up and said, "But I don't believe the Bible." It is important, you see, to know something about where to begin in our teaching. Paul knew that Felix was an unjust man, lacking in self control, and unprepared for the judgment. Therefore he reasoned with him of these things (Acts 24:25). Ananias knew that Saul believed in Christ, there was much evidence he had repented and the thing he needed to do was to be baptized (Acts 22:16).

At the conclusion of Peter's formal discourse on Pentecost (Acts 2), he got some response from the audience (v. 37). He then proceeded to answer their question by telling them what they must do to escape the consequences of their sin. There are times when we need to get some student response so we will know how to proceed with the teaching.

Another technique we can observe in the New Testament is that of correcting false concepts. It is obvious that the scribes and Pharisees had a false concept about the commandments of the Lord concerning their traditions (Matt. 15:1-14). Jesus corrected this false concept and showed them they were making the commandments of God "of none effect" (v. 6) by their tradition. Priscilla and Aquila used this technique when they heard Apollos preaching the baptism of John after it had been superseded by the baptism of Christ in the great commission. The Bible says "they took him unto them and taught him the way of the Lord more perfectly" (Acts 18:26).

The Bible truly is a teacher-training manual, the inspired one.

DISCUSSION ACTIVITIES

1. Small-group activity: Let each group look at the example of Christ teaching the Samaritan woman at the well in John 4. Make a list of the different techniques of teaching Jesus used in just this one example of teaching. See which group can find the most; report the findings back to the total group.

2. Class discussion: Discuss Paul's approach to teaching the people on Mars' hill in Acts 17. Why didn't he tell about Abraham? Baptism? The work of the church?

3. Individual activity: Look at Matthew 5-7 and count how many words, expressions and concepts are used to make points (such things as salt, candles, light, etc.). Why did Jesus go to all this trouble to make His points? Weren't the people intelligent enough to understand Him otherwise? What about us today?

4. In 2 Samuel 12, Nathan had a message for David. Discuss as a class how he went about getting this message across to David. Who finally drew the conclusion, Nathan or David? How is this used as a teaching technique today?

5. Small-group activity: Let each group find examples where anyone in the Bible answered a question with a question. Discuss the results they got from this teaching method. Does it still work today?

> Col. 4:6
> Let your speech be alway with grace, seasoned with salt, that ye may know how ye ought to answer every man.

CHAPTER 3

SOME BASIC PROBLEMS IN BIBLE TEACHING

1 Cor. 9:16

For though I preach the gospel, I have nothing to glory of: for necessity is laid upon me, yea, woe is unto me, if I preach not the gospel!

Lack Of Desire To Teach Can Be A Problem

It is difficult to understand why a person who has been taught of God and has become a Christian would not want to teach others the way of salvation, but the fact remains that many do not want to be teachers. It occurs to us that many are lacking in a desire to teach because they are convinced that someone else would make a better teacher than they would. Did you ever stop to analyze that line of reasoning? Let's look at it for a moment. Would you apply it to every phase of your life? Is the reason you do not play golf, bowl, fish, or engage in some other recreation, particularly a competitive sport, because someone else is better at it than you are? Husbands, suppose your wife said she was not going to cook any more because she was not as good a cook as someone else? You wives have not stopped cooking because you are not as good at it as someone else, have you? Now we are well aware there is much more at stake in teaching the word of God than in recreation, or even in teaching, but we are also aware that the Lord expects us to do the best we can in teaching what we know of His word and improving ourselves as we study and put into practice what we learn.

Some have a lack of a desire to teach because they feel they cannot teach at all. Certainly there are some who are better teachers than others, and perhaps there are a few who absolutely cannot stand before certain groups in a class teaching situation and teach a Bible lesson. But we are equally persuaded that a great many of those who say they cannot really could if they decided this is what they wanted to do. The Lord does not expect us to do what we cannot do, but He does expect us to use and develop the talents He has given us, and in fact will hold us accountable for such. Read Matthew 25:14-30.

One of the things which causes some not to desire to be teachers of the word of God is fear. Some are afraid of the criticism they may receive from others and consequently do not want to teach. Some will refuse to accept the responsibility of teaching for this very reason. If everyone who ever received criticism for something they said or did in their teaching suddenly decided not to teach any more there would not be very much teaching done. Those who teach are human and do make mistakes which need to be corrected, and constructive criticism needs to be offered. Critics do not always know how, nor do they always exercise wisdom and good judgment in offering their criticism, but Christians should not allow this to discourage us to the point of not becoming teachers or of quitting after we have become involved in this all-important work.

A humble Christian of our acquaintance, with a limited formal education, was teaching a lesson in a Bible class when the local church was disturbed over a fundamental principle. In his efforts to show the teaching of the scriptures on the point at hand he misspelled a simple word on the board. An influential man in the congregation publicly criticized and ridiculed him before the class saying that he was not qualified to teach. While this kind of an attack hurt the teacher very deeply it did not hinder him from using his ability to teach and his influence to encourage people to accept the truth of God.

Some Are Afraid Of Questions

Some hesitate to teach because they are afraid someone will ask a question they will not be able to answer. When we consider the different motives people have for asking questions – and the many questions that can be put to a teacher- we can certainly recognize that no one would be expected to come up with the correct answer to every question that may be put to him. There are some suggestions which should help overcome this fear, however. The teacher should always encourage the students to ask only the questions that will enable them to learn the truth, and let it be known that those questions which engender strife and confusion will not be considered. One can learn a great deal about answering questions by studying the example of Jesus. It is certainly true that we cannot look into the heart of another and know what his motive is for asking a particular question as Jesus did, but we can learn how to answer his question with a question and thereby place the responsibility of answering his question on him. This oftentimes brings out the motive for asking the question: whether the querist is sincerely seeking the Bible answer or is trying to trap the teacher.

There are some students who will ask questions for the purpose of getting the teacher to spend the entire class period telling them the answer. This diverts the attention away from the lesson assigned for that class period and lets the student shift his mind into "neutral" while the teacher lectures to the class. Usually questions of this type are asked to occupy time and not out of a desire to know the truth on the subject, and keep the student from becoming involved in class participation and the learning process. It is not always easy to know what motive prompts a student to ask a question, but it helps to prevent questions being asked for the purpose of wasting time, as well as helping to learn better the answers, to place a lot of the responsibility of finding the answers on the students themselves.

It is not a disgrace to be asked a Bible question to which you do not know the answer, but if it is a matter of concern and importance to the person asking it then an effort should be made to find the answer and report back at the next class meeting. This can be a means of getting participation from the class, i.e., by assigning the class the responsibility of finding the answer and then by beginning the next class period with a discussion of what they learned about it. So you see there can be worse things for a teacher than not being able to answer all the questions the students might ask.

Teaching Requires Too Much Effort

There are those who decline to accept the responsibility of becoming a teacher because they are unwilling to put forth the effort and spend the time necessary to prepare. It is a fact that it takes time and effort to be a successful teacher of the word of God and those who are unwilling to face up to this reality will never become good teachers. Teaching is a skill and people do not become skillful simply by wishing or inactivity, but by proper application of methods which will develop the skill. If people put forth no more effort in learning the skill to enable them to perform the duties assigned them on their job than many do to develop the skill of teaching the word of God to others, how many would be able to keep their jobs? Business men require that the people they hire prove their qualifications for the job and/or show willingness to learn how to be proficient at it, putting forth the effort necessary to prepare for it. Yet in the Church many who are given the solemn responsibility of guiding the destinies of the souls of others put little time in learning what to teach them and even less in learning how best to enable their students to learn life's most important lessons.

Oftentimes when people in the church are approached and asked to teach or encouraged to prepare themselves to teach they begin to offer excuses such as "I can't teach," "some one else can do that better than I can," "I don't have time to prepare" or some such when in reality a lack of desire to teach is back of it. Desiring to be teachers while understanding neither what we say nor whereof we affirm (1 Tim. 1:7) is not the right thing to do, but the Bible does tell Christians to be apt to teach (2 Tim. 2:24). All Christians should desire to teach for the good they can do in saving souls.

Lack Of Good Teacher-Training Programs Is A Problem

Another basic problem in Bible teaching is the lack of good teacher-training programs. In many local churches there seems to be little or no program for the purpose of training people to be better teachers.

Perhaps one of the reasons there are so few good teacher-training programs being conducted is the failure to see the importance of such. Many seem to think that as long as we have classes with a fair number of people in attendance and someone to act as the teacher, that is all that is needed. We don't reason that way about those who teach our children in the public schools, but for some unexplained reason we do not seem to place as much importance upon having qualified teachers in the Bible classes.

Some members of the Lord's church have a lethargic attitude to teacher-training programs in a local church, and when elders plan a special series of lessons for the purpose of developing more and better teachers many do not avail themselves of the opportunity to participate. Obviously good teacher-training programs must have people who want to learn to improve themselves as well as those who will plan and conduct them. There need to be more leaders who have the vision to plan and conduct programs designed to improve the teaching of the Bible and there need to be more who will show an interest by attending such.

To have a successful teacher-training program there must not only be a desire to have such a program and a willingness to plan and conduct such, but there must also be some one who is qualified to do so to teach such a class. A good teacher-training program involves much more than having a meeting of the teachers once a month and/or a class in teacher-training periodically. It includes having leaders in the congregation who will have a desire to build up the church and recognize the necessity of sound teaching in accomplishing this goal. Teachers, like heroes, are made, not born. Hence the need of having a continuous good teacher-training program. Periodic teacher-training sessions can serve a good purpose in a local congregation as gospel meetings can and do.

Teachers Must Deal With Under-Motivated Students

Often when someone mentions something about motivating students to study the Bible, about the only thing some can think of is giving them candy, refreshments and the like. On the other hand there are those who believe the only motivation one needs for Bible study is the realization of the fact that it is the Bible. Students of all ages need proper motivation in learning at each class period discussion as well as in reaching the ultimate goal of eternal life. Appealing to a student's natural competitive spirit, his desire to excel, his demonstration of his ability to learn, can be as successful in getting him to learn important Bible principles as promising him a star if he attends every class meeting for a quarter, or says his memory verse every Sunday. Promising a reward is not the only way to motivate students to learn, and neither is the fear of punishment.

When students are under-motivated they often lose interest in learning, attend the classes infrequently, become discipline problems, disturb the class and hinder others from learning. One of the most stimulating and exciting ways to motivate students to learn is through the process of discovering something hitherto unknown to that person. Discovering a new idea, like discovering new territory on land, sea, or in space, increases one's desire to learn, and consequently motivates him to more diligent study.

Improper Physical Facilities
Can Hinder The Teacher

Did you ever try to hold the attention and teach a Bible lesson to a dozen boys (or girls) in a cluttered storage room of a building used for kindergarten, girl scouts, baby health center, voting place, as well as for religious services? Perhaps you say this is an exaggerated situation, but it has happened (to me), and it is much more difficult to get the lesson across than with proper physical facilities. Let me hasten to say that it is possible to have all the latest and best equipment available and still not be successful as a Bible teacher. However, a skillful teacher will be much more successful with proper physical facilities than without them.

One of the problems in teaching where physical facilities are concerned is in deciding exactly what facilities are needed and procuring and using them. In most places people are convinced that certain things such as chalkboards, tack boards, flannel boards, maps, etc., are needed in teaching situations, but many times even the teachers do not know just what they need nor how to make proper use of what they do have. A part of the problem is in the general appearance of the room itself. Teachers should make an effort to have the room as cheerful as possible, and should have things arranged so as to cause the students to be glad to be there, and to want to learn. The teacher is greatly handicapped who does not have facilities, through means of which the students actually become involved in the learning process and through the use of which the application of spiritual truth becomes a personal reality. To derive benefit from a study of the Bible we must make application to our own lives and this involves knowing how to make that application. Careful consideration should be given to what physical facilities are available and what are needed, and how to make the proper use of them in teaching the truth.

Lack Of Parental Concern Can Cause Problems

This problem in teaching has to do primarily with children. When teachers have as their students those whose parents have no more concern for their attending Bible classes than the opportunity of getting them out of the house for an hour or so, those teachers have problems and the chances of the students learning very much is pretty slim. It is a true statement that Bible class teachers get some students in their classes whose parents really have little or no concern as to whether their children learn very much about the Bible or not. There seems to be an attitude among some parents that they want their children to attend some Bible classes so they will be able to say in later life that they used to attend Bible school.

Obviously this kind of situation presents a problem for teachers, for the teacher must provide most if not all the motivation for the student to learn. Sometimes it is possible for the child to get the parents involved by the enthusiasm he may show in the things he has learned. Truly there are times when "a little child shall lead them" (Isa. 11:6).

Students' Lack Of Bible Knowledge May Be A Problem

It would be a rare situation if an entire class of eleven- and twelve year-old students, for example, had the same general knowledge of the Bible. That this presents a problem in effective Bible teaching is quite evident when the teacher, telling such stories as Jonah and the whale, suggests that the students read the account for themselves, then sees them thumb through the Bible in search of the book of Jonah, not knowing whether it is in the New Testament or the Old Testament. This problem not only exists among children, but among adults as well. When a small percentage of the students in a Bible class have such a limited knowledge of the Bible that the teacher must explain every point in detail the rest of the members of the class have a tendency to lose interest as they want to move along more rapidly in the learning process.

Since in most local congregations it is not expedient to divide the classes into slower and more advanced groups, as is sometimes done in public school systems, the teacher must find ways to stimulate and involve the whole class. Quizzing the class to determine the point at which each member has progressed in Bible knowledge and then assigning the students work according to their capabilities is one way to overcome this problem. Another suggestion that proves to be helpful is assigning group activities, putting at least one person in each group who is more advanced in Bible knowledge with some who are somewhat limited so he can help bring them to a greater degree of knowledge and understanding.

Teachers have the responsibility of recognizing problems when they exist and of seeking solutions to them. Jesus said, "For ye have the poor with you always..." (Mark 14:7), and this seems to be true of problems also. They will not go away by ignoring them, but they can be overcome.

DISCUSSION ACTIVITIES

1. Two-group activity: Have one group list all the reasons they can remember that they have heard from people who were trying to get out of teaching (mostly, these will be excuses). Have the other group list justifiable reasons why a person could refuse to teach a class. When each is through, list their findings side by side on the board. Do any of them match?

2. Class discussion: What is the best answer to give to someone who uses the excuses given in the answer to Question 1?

3. Class discussion: How can a person overcome the problem of not being able to speak in front of a group? Are there other ways of teaching besides in front of a large audience? What are some of them (more than just personal work)?

4. Group project: In whatever way you decide to work on it, come up with a satisfactory teacher-training program for a congregation of average size. Decide how to build the interest for the class, how to encourage those who haven't taught before to attend, what the course goals are, etc.

5. Now look at the course designed above and decide how to keep training going so that new teachers continue to be developed, and experienced ones continue to update their methods. (This is a harder task than in Question 4!)

> Acts 2:40
> And with many other words did he testify and exhort, saying, Save yourselves from this untoward generation.

CHAPTER 4

SOME ADVANTAGES IN BIBLE TEACHING

1 Tim. 4:16
Take heed unto thyself, and unto the doctrine; continue in them: for in doing this thou shalt both save thyself, and them that hear thee.

Although there are admittedly problems in Bible teaching, there are also some advantages. A closer look at them will encourage the beginning Bible teacher.

The Message Does Not Change

In every course in secular education textbooks must be revised frequently and new ones written from time to time because the message changes as new information is learned. But this is not true with the teaching of the Bible. God's final and complete revelation to man in the New Testament scriptures is as fresh and as applicable today as when it was given in the first century. The apostle Peter said that the Lord has given us "all things that pertain unto life and godliness" (2 Pet. 1:3); and the apostle Paul affirmed that the scriptures inspired of God are "profitable for doctrine, for reproof, for correction, for instruction in righteousness: That the man of God may be perfect, thoroughly furnished unto all good works" (2 Tim. 3: 16-17). Not only do these passages indicate the finality of the New Testament scriptures, but Jude told us the faith "was once (for all – ASV) delivered unto the saints" (Jude 3) which would also indicate the finality of it.

The above scriptures show that God has given us the final revelation of His will to man and therefore *will not change it.* We now consider some passages which show that *man is forbidden to change God's message.* The curse of heaven is promised to all who pervert the gospel and preach any message other than that which the apostles preached (Gal. 1:8-9), and which they have written (1 Cor. 14:37). To transgress or go beyond and abide not in the doctrine of Christ brings God's disapproval (2 John 9-11). The apostle Peter *added* that those who wrest the scriptures (twist or change them about) do so to their own destruction (2 Pet. 3:16). Not only does God forbid the changing of the New Testament, but He did not permit the people to change the Old Testament when it was in force (Deut. 4:2).

The Message Is Clear And Simple

The Bible teaches "that God is no respecter of persons: But in every Nation he that feareth him, and worketh righteousness, is accepted with him" (Acts 10:34-35). The God who gave us the Bible does not want us to be lost (2 Pet. 3:9), but has said that all who do not obey His will "shall be punished with everlasting destruction" (2 Thess. 1:7-9). He requires that we understand and do His will in order to be saved. Therefore we know it is possible for us to understand it if we have the proper attitude toward it. Consider the clear and simple way in which Jesus taught the people in parables, using things with which they were familiar to teach them about the deeper spiritual matters.

The Message Itself Is Motivating

Whether we realize it or not the need for motivating students to learn is as great today as it has ever been. The problem with many teachers is in knowing where to look for this motivation and then how to motivate the students to learn. There is a great deal more motivation for learning in the message of the Bible than many of us have found. We assume those in our Bible classes believe the Bible is the inspired word of God. Who among such students would not be motivated to learn all he could about God's wonderful creation simply by reading the account given of the creation in the first two chapters of Genesis? Likewise the message of God's plan of redemption for man (which is the real message of the Bible) is presented in the Bible so as to cause the sincere person to want to know all he can about this plan that he may follow it and receive the blessings promised therein. The message in the crucifixion of Jesus motivates people to want to know why He died.

There Is Something For All Ages

Children thrill to the stories of Jochebed and Moses, Hannah and Samuel, David and Goliath, and many others. The stories of the destruction of the world by water in Noah's day, the destruction of Sodom and Gomorrah by fire and brimstone from heaven can be made to come alive and young people can thereby be motivated to learn what a terrible thing sin is in the eyes of God as well as how they may escape from its punishment.

Adults can be motivated to learn by the statements which show the value of the spiritual over the material or physical –

indicating the danger of putting our trust in the uncertainty of riches, and the reward promised to those who lay up for themselves treasures in heaven. There is also something in the Bible for the aged to learn how to grow old gracefully as they view their departure from this earth, not as the end of all things for them, but, if they have served the Lord faithfully and died in Him, as an opportunity to go and be with Him and to rest from their labors (Phil. 1:21-23; 2 Tim. 4:6-8; Rev. 14:13).

There Is Something For Any Condition Or Station In Life

One of the truly great advantages of Bible teaching is the fact that whether you are teaching the rich or poor, learned or unlearned, imprisoned or free, kings or subjects, there is a message there for them. The rich man can learn how to use his wealth to benefit himself and others and the poor man can learn how to be a worthwhile servant of God by being content with such things as he has and using them in the service of God. The apostles went to the rulers with the message of salvation and they also went to the poor. Jesus could talk to the shepherds about the Great Shepherd of His sheep, to farmers about sowing the seed and reaping the fruit at the harvest, to fishermen about how to become fishers of men, to the wealthy about the danger of putting their trust in uncertain riches and of laying up for themselves treasures in heaven, to the poor about the riches in the Father's storehouse, to the thirsty about the water of life which when a person drinks he will never thirst again, to the masters about the honor and value of true service, and to all the value of the spiritual over the material.

There Is No Greater Personal Reward For Success

The apostle John wrote, "I have no greater joy than to hear that my children walk in truth" (3 John 4). Surely this expresses the feeling all faithful Bible teachers have toward those whom they have taught the word of the Lord. But there is not only the joy that one feels in this life in knowing those he has taught are walking in the truth of the gospel, there is also an eternal reward in heaven. Paul told Timothy to "Take heed unto thyself, and unto the doctrine; continue in them: for in doing this thou shalt both save thyself, and them that hear thee" (1 Tim. 4:16). Regardless of how great the reward may be for engaging in some successful endeavor in this life none could compare with the reward of everlasting life in heaven with God.

DISCUSSION ACTIVITIES

1. The Bible is often called a history book. As a class discussion decide what the difference is between teaching ancient history of the secular world and Bible history.

2. The Bible is also called a science book. In the same fashion as in Question 1, discuss the difference between teaching modern science and the science of the Bible.

3. The Bible is sometimes called a book of psychology and philosophy. Have half the class come up with a list of "Philosophies" taught in the Bible, while the other half lists examples of the use of psychology in the Bible. Report the findings back to the group as a whole.

4. With the Bible as proof-text prepare a debate between two groups on the question "Human nature never changes." (The negative group will have to draw most of its argument from man's logic.)

5. Group discussion: Why is it that men today still look for further revelation from God? What would be the consequence if even one person received an additional message from God? What would happen to such passages as Jude 3, 2 Timothy 3:16-17, 2 Peter 1:3?

> Acts 16:32-34
> And they spake unto him the word of the Lord, and to all that were in his house. And he took them the same hour of the night, and washed their stripes; and was baptized, he and all his, straightway. And when he had brought them into his house, he set meat before them, and rejoiced. believing in God with all his house.

CHAPTER 5

SOME DANGERS IN BIBLE TEACHING

James 3:1
My brethren, be not many teachers (ASV), knowing that we shall receive the greater condemnation.

Just as surely as there are advantages in Bible teaching there are some dangers of which we must beware. One does not have to allow the presence of dangers to discourage him from becoming a teacher, nor should they be allowed to become pitfalls in our pathway to becoming better Bible teachers.

Teaching Has Greater Accountability

As we have already stated in the previous chapter teachers shall receive greater condemnation or heavier judgment (James 3:1). Teachers have greater accountability because of the greatness of their responsibility – dealing with the eternal destiny of the precious souls of those whom they teach.

Some students learn very little about the Bible other than what they get from their teachers in Bible classes. Since impressions that are made in the classroom are usually lasting ones teachers need to be careful to make truthful impressions. Jesus emphasized to His disciples the danger of following blind guides. He said, "And if the blind lead the blind, both shall fall into the ditch" (Matt. 15:14).

This does not minimize the responsibility of those who are being led by the blind guides, but it does emphasize the greatness of the responsibility of those who lead in spiritual matters.

Our Lives Must Be Exemplary

"Don't do as I do, but do as I say do" does not have its basis in the life and teaching of Jesus Christ, nor any sound principle of teaching. People are great imitators. Therefore example is one of the best ways of teaching others. The New Testament writers, especially the apostle Paul, frequently mentioned the value of example by reminding the people of the way he had behaved in their presence, and how they should follow him as he followed Christ (2 Thess. 3:7; 1 Cor. 11:1).

Elders, preachers, yea all Christians, are to be examples. Paul warned the elders of the church of Ephesus to take heed to themselves as well as to the flock. According to Hebrews 13:7 we should follow the faith of those who have the rule over us, and Peter said that elders are to be examples (1 Pet. 5:3). In one of Paul's letters to Timothy he pointed out that he should be an example of those who believe (1 Tim. 4:12).

The one from whom we best learn by example is Jesus Christ. Luke wrote that He "began both to do and teach" (Acts 1:1). He exemplified what He wanted of His followers by doing always the things that pleased the Father (John 8:29). The apostle Peter told us plainly that Jesus left us "an example, that ye should follow his steps" (1 Pet. 2:21). Perhaps the statement in the Bible that best expresses the exemplary life the teacher is to live is the one in which Paul admonished

Timothy to "Take heed unto thyself, and unto the doctrine; continue in them: for in doing this thou shalt both save thyself, and them that hear thee" (1 Tim. 4:16). What right does the teacher, whether he or she be parent, elder, preacher, Bible class teacher, have to expect of the student that which he or she is unwilling to do?

The Message Must Not Change

We have mentioned some statements from the Bible which indicate to us the everlasting consequences which await those who change the message of the scriptures. One of the dangers facing Bible teachers is the tendency to change that message on some particular point to suit ourselves or someone of our acquaintance. The consequence is not earth-shaking when a teacher changes the message somewhat in teaching a course in history, language, or some such secular subject, but the eternal destiny of the souls of both teacher and students is involved in Bible teaching. For this reason the Bible teacher must be constantly aware of the danger of changing the message.

The gospel of Christ is God's remedy for the disease of sin, and there must be no change in the prescription He gave if the cure is to be affected. When the doctor writes out a prescription for the cure of a disease he found in our body we do not want the pharmacist to change even one ingredient. As Bible teachers we should be alert lest we inadvertently change the message and thereby lose our own souls and cause others to be lost also.

Error Invades Unawares

Regardless of how careful teachers are in presenting the truth and urging the students to adhere strictly to it, there is always the danger of error getting in. We can observe in the New Testament scriptures that this was true with Christ and the apostles even as it is true today. Jesus warned His disciples to "Beware of false prophets, which come to you in sheep's clothing, but inwardly they are ravening wolves" (Matt. 7:15), and the wolves did come among them with their false doctrines. The apostle John tells Christians to "try the spirits whether they are of God: because many false prophets are gone out into the world" (1 John 4:1). Other similar warnings are given in the holy scriptures and they are needed as much today as they were when they were first given. For this reason Bible teachers need to know the teaching of the Bible so they can recognize *error* when it is taught and be able to help their students to recognize it also.

The devil is very subtle in the way he mixes error in with the truth. For this reason the danger facing the Bible teacher is not only in being able to detect the error himself, but in helping the *students to recognize and refute it* when it appears. The teacher will not always be around when the student is faced with some religious error. Therefore the student should be shown how to recognize the difference between what the Bible teaches and what men teach. Various techniques which will accomplish this are discussed elsewhere in this book, but it should be pointed out here that it is the responsibility of the teacher to get the students involved in discovering the difference for themselves by actually studying some doctrines and proving by the Bible whether they are true or not.

Truth Always Has Opposition

One cannot study the life and teaching of Jesus Christ without being impressed with the fact that the truth always has opposition. Both among the Jews and the Romans there were those who did not believe the truth Jesus taught and they opposed it with vigor. John told us that "He (Jesus) came unto His own, and His own received Him not" (John 1:11). Jesus prepared His disciples for the same kind of opposition by telling them, "If they have persecuted me, they will persecute you; if they have kept my saying, they will keep yours also" (John 15:20b).

The preaching of the apostle Paul in various places also indicates that the truth has opposition. Frequently he was allowed to preach in the Jewish synagogues until he taught them that the Jewish system of religion, including the sabbath commandment, had been taken out of the way and Christ had given us a new law. Because of their opposition to the truth he was forced to do his teaching elsewhere. Even when he was forced to leave one city and flee to another to preserve his life, such as Thessalonica (Acts 17:10), or stoned and left for dead, as in Lystra (Acts 14:19), he did not cease his preaching.

These are but two of the many Bible examples illustrating the fact that truth has opposition. The lesson for us to learn from this is that we cannot fail to teach the truth even though there is opposition. When we come to the full realization that it takes the truth to free men from sin (John 8:32), we will not allow opposition to it to keep us from teaching it to others.

Error Can Be Taught Innocently

Not everyone who teaches error sets out to do so deliberately. It is possible for one to teach error without knowing that it is error. Apollos was an eloquent man and mighty in the scriptures, but he knew only the baptism of John until Priscilla and Aquila took him aside and taught him the way of the Lord more accurately (Acts 18:24-26). Paul was in ignorance when he was opposing Christ (1 Tim. 1:13). There are doubtless a great number of people today who believe they are teaching the truth, but who are in reality teaching error. For this reason Bible teachers continually need to take heed unto ourselves and the doctrine that we may be able to save ourselves and others (1 Tim. 4:16).

The responsibility of Bible teachers is great. Our own souls are at stake and so are the souls of those we teach. Therefore we need to know the difference between the truth which saves (John 8:32; 1 Pet. 1:22) and the errors of men which damn the soul (2 Thess. 2:10-12). We also need to help our students to be able to make this distinction and follow truth in the face of all opposition.

Problems arise in Bible teaching, but with the help of the Lord and the use of His infallible guide, the Bible, they are not insurmountable.

DISCUSSION ACTIVITIES

1. Group discussion: Without naming names or making it so the group can identify the people being discussed, think of teachers you have known in the past who were good

teachers but had personal habits that were not exemplary of Christian teachers. Discuss: "After all, if a person can teach the Bible, that's the important thing. Regardless of his personal life, the message is still getting there" (2 Thess. 3:7; 1 Cor. 11:1).

2. Obviously teachers should get in the habit of using scriptures to prove that what they are teaching is from God's word. As a group, discuss what habits a *student* should develop along these same lines. Should a teacher encourage a student to question whether a thing is taught in the scripture or not? After all, the teacher wouldn't be teaching the subject if he wasn't sure it was right. (What does the Bible have to say about the relationship between the teacher and the student? 1 John 4:1.)

3. Group discussion: Why is it that truth always seems to have opposition? Why aren't people glad to find the truth? We hear so much about the "search for truth."

4. What part does the devil play in disguising error? How do we know? (See scripture references in this chapter.)

5. Group debate: With the class divided into two halves, debate the following: "If students don't want to hear the truth, then we ought not to waste our time. After all, they ought to know that their souls are at stake."

> Acts 18:26
> And he began to speak boldly in the synagogue: whom when Aquila and Priscilla had heard, they took him unto them, and expounded unto him the way of God more perfectly.

PART II

TEACHING TECHNIQUES

CHAPTERS 6-7

CHAPTER 6

BASIC PRINCIPLES OF LEARNING

Acts 8:30-31
And Philip ran thither to him, and heard him read the prophet Isaiah, and said, Understandest thou what thou readest? And he said, How can I, except some man should guide me? And he desired Philip that he would come up and sit with him.

There are some "first principles" of learning that are simple to understand, essential to learning, easy to do, obvious when explained, *yet very frequently ignored* by most teachers. In this chapter we will talk about them. Later we will see the application.

Involvement Is Necessary

All learning is self-activity. I learn for myself; no one can learn for me. If I listen to a lecture, I decide if I'm going to go to the trouble of opening my ears, letting my brain think about the subject. The teacher may be doing very well at "covering" the material, but he cannot learn for me, nor even force me to remain mentally involved – *as long as he just lectures.*

The successful teacher, at any class level, doesn't depend entirely upon the student to get involved. He prepares activities that force involvement (or at least make it easier). His teaching techniques are conscious efforts to encourage involvement. He knows that learning takes place only when the learner is involved, so he does those things that cause involvement.

Learning Motivates Learning

Teachers often ask, "What can I do to motivate my students to learn?" One answer is so simple it's often overlooked: *Let them learn!* Few things reward us as much as knowing we have actually learned something. This is true at any age. But notice, we said *knowing* we have learned. It isn't enough just to suspect that we have learned something; we must know it for sure to be motivated to continue to seek new learning experiences. Later we'll see how to accomplish this, that is, we'll see how the teacher can be sure the student knows he's learned. For now, let's just be sure to understand that if we expect to use learning as a motivator, we'll have to let the learner in on the fact.

This gives us another reason for involving the student: to let him find out he has learned something. The tricky part of learning is that we aren't always aware of whether or not we have learned. We hear a reference or a scripture and think we have committed it to memory. We hear several excellent points and think we won't forget them. Then we start to use this information and find that it is no longer available to us – we simply can't recall it. It's important to note that at the time we heard the information we understood it. We knew what the teacher was saying, it made sense, we agreed with it and for a short while at least, we were mentally involved. We had every reason to believe we *had learned* the subject. But it had only gotten into our "short term memory" and had not become a part of anything long term.

The Teacher Has The Responsibility

The teacher, then, has a responsibility to the student – in the process used in teaching – to see that involvement is present. When students seem to have no desire to learn, the teacher needs to ask, "Am I giving the student an opportunity to *know* he has learned?" Does he know that he has learned something he didn't know, something that is useful, something that he can repeat with confidence? This is one of the benefits of drills; the student is getting feedback on himself. He knows how well he's doing towards learning. If the student shows a lack of interest, the teacher has a responsibility to see if this is a symptom of something the *teacher* is doing wrong. Is the teacher failing to let the students in on the learning exercise? Have the students just decided that they aren't really needed in the classroom because the teacher is going on without them anyway? An alert teacher will always ask, "Could this class have been run without the students?" If the answer is "Yes" then there is a good chance not much was learned. Certainly the students didn't know they had learned anything.

This doesn't mean that *only* the teacher has the responsibility for what happens in the classroom. The students should be interested in what goes on, they should want to learn, they should be accountable for their own actions-but it is the teacher's responsibility first, then the students'. The teacher sets the climate for learning. He lets the students know whether or not they are going to be a part of the class activity or are going to be expected to sit quietly while the teacher demonstrates how much he knows about the subject.

Unfortunately, the relationship between the teacher and learner sometimes becomes a sparring contest. The teacher is more concerned with discipline than with learning, with the group being quiet than with them participating. When this happens, there is little hope for learning. The teacher says to himself, "As soon as they get quiet, I'll start teaching." The students say, "As soon as he starts to do something interesting we'll get quiet."

Feedback Is Essential

The key to successful learning is the quantity and quality *of feedback* that gets to both the teacher and the learner. This is just a fancy way of saying that the students need to know where they are and the teacher does too. The more feedback there is the more each can adjust to the situation. If the students know where they're supposed to be going and they discover they aren't getting there, they can change their habits. If the teacher expects certain results and isn't getting them, he knows that adjustments must be made. But it's too late to find this out at the end of the class period or the end of a quarter.

To accomplish anything worthwhile, both the student and the learner must have frequent, reliable information as to what learning is taking place. All of this says that there must be participation, involvement, activity on the part of the students. Feedback is obtained when the student is doing something. If he is doing something that demonstrates what learning has taken place, both he and the teacher know this. If this comes early enough in the class period, they both can do something about it. If the feedback comes at the end of the session, it's too late to do much but worry about the next class period. This means that good teachers will try to get as much feedback as early as possible so they can make whatever adjustments are needed. The idea is to present some new information, cause involvement, assure ourselves that the students are getting the information, then go to the next point. This not only keeps us informed but is much more interesting and reassuring to the students. In the next chapter we will see some of the simple ways in which feedback can be gotten.

Help The Learner Remember

An interesting thing about the learning process is that students don't always know what is good or bad for them. For example, we sometimes think it would be good for the teacher just to tell us the answer or give us the conclusion. Most teachers think this is a pretty good idea, too. But all the evidence we have on how we remember shows that we remember the things we say – especially the conclusions we reach – much longer than the conclusions or things we hear *someone* else say. This means that the effective teacher will quit just before the conclusion, rather than just *after* he has given it. The difference seems insignificant, but in the long run, the student will benefit considerably from the things he says.

The idea of the student coming up with the conclusion isn't difficult to understand. When the teacher does all the work, all the student has to do is use his sense of hearing, try to find a place to store the information and forget about it. He doesn't have to think about it, worry with it, solve any problems or draw on any other part of his brain; all he has to do is receive it. On the other hand, when the student has to come up with a conclusion on his own – based on information given him by the teacher – he has to go to other parts of his brain. He has to recall the information already given him. He has to do some analyzing. He has to check his thinking against the instructor, perhaps having to ask a question to clear up a point he doesn't understand (something he probably wouldn't have had to do if the instructor were doing all the talking), In the process of going through all the mental motions, there is no wonder that the student retains a lot more of what has been going on.

It Is Not A Game

The process we're talking about here isn't one of the instructor playing "Hot or Cold" with the student. The instructor gives the students enough clues to cause them to come up with the correct conclusion. If the students don't come up with the conclusion immediately, more clues are given. The teacher may even ask a question or two to stimulate the students' thinking along the right channels. We might call this process or technique the "Discovery System," since it allows the student to discover the truth or the conclusion. In this connection, let's look at some various levels of teaching and see where this system fits.

First, there is the Direct Teacher Input System. In this system all the new information and all the conclusions come from the teacher. The student is passive throughout the entire process, except that he may be given some questions at the end of the study period "to see how well he did." (In reality, many times it shows how poorly the teacher did!) In this system, there is no feedback, either to the teacher or the student. Success depends entirely on the skill of the teacher in getting each point made, and the skill of the student in keeping all the information stored properly. Much is left to chance. The lecture method of teaching is the best example of this, but even a movie or a filmstrip with sound falls in the same category. The *teaching process is all one-way.*

The next level above this is the Teacher Modification System. In this system, the teacher gets feedback from the student, but only on that which the teacher has been instructing. The teacher still reaches all the conclusions and presents all the information, but the student at least participates enough for the teacher to see whether or not his message has gotten through. An obvious example of this is any kind of question and answer exercise, providing the questions are over material already covered. Remember, in this system, the student isn't coming up with any of the conclusions – the teacher is putting out all of the new information, coming to all of the conclusions and only asking the student questions to test the teacher's effectiveness at teaching and the student's effectiveness at learning. This is a much improved system over the Direct Teacher Input System because it allows for feedback to the teacher, and a chance for the student to test the knowledge he has gained. The involvement that is obtained helps the student remember, because just repeating the answers helps a lot. This isn't as much mental involvement as he would get if he came to the conclusions himself, but it's better than no involvement at all.

The system we mentioned earlier in this chapter – the Discovery System – allows the student to use his mind to a greater degree by using some information to reach a conclusion for himself. Studies show that we remember things a lot longer and a lot better if we do the mental work to come to the conclusions ourselves. The way this works is that the teacher provides enough information to lead to the conclusion, but the student still has to do some mental exercising to see where the information leads. Christ used this method constantly, asking questions and letting the listener come to his own conclusion. Most of the time when we answer a question with a question, we are using this method.

By the way, it isn't so important that we remember a name of a method or technique; the important thing is that we recognize that some techniques aid the learning process more than others, and we use those techniques most often. The problem arises in that we can't always tell that a particular method is being used. For example, when a person is teaching and asks a question, we have to know what's been going on to tell whether or not he's asking questions on something that already has been discussed, or whether he's asking the students to come to their own conclusions. The observer can't tell, but the learner can, and the difference in his recall later is going to be tremendous. There are various studies on how well we remember things, and the amount we remember of what we hear doesn't compare at all favorably with what we remember of what we say. Most studies show that we remember about 20 per cent of what we hear as compared to 70 per cent of what we say – providing we're *arriving at a conclusion* when we say the thing to be remembered.

Conclusion

All of this says that there are some effective ways of teaching and some ineffective ways. Those methods that are the most successful somehow get the learner involved; get him reaching conclusions on his own and get him to be the center of the instruction. Too many classes could be taught without the students, if the teacher could somehow be fooled into thinking that there were "warm bodies" out there. In all of this, there must be some feedback to both the student and the teacher, so that each will not only know that learning has taken place, but also that the *right* learning has transpired. No teaching- learning is complete until we know this!

DISCUSSION ACTIVITIES

1. Small-group discussion: Have several small groups discuss the following statement for several minutes. "Learning is one of the best motivations to further learning." Each group should come up with at least two positive examples of how this works. These should be reported back to the entire group and discussed.

2. Two-group discussion: Divide the group into two groups. Have one of them discuss and list all the reasons why a teacher needs to get feedback on his teaching activities (during class). The other group should discuss and make a list of all the reasons why a student should get feedback during a teaching-learning process.

3. Two-group activity: Let one half of the group list all the things they like about teachers. Let the other half of the group list all the things they like about students. Record these side by side on the board. Now have the group as a

whole discuss these, seeing if any of the things the teachers do that are good could cause students to perform well.

4. Use the same arrangement as above. One group should list the things they don't like about the teachers, the other should list things they don't like about students. As in Question 3, record and see if anything the teachers do could cause the actions of the students.

5. Group discussion: Think of examples of teachers in the Bible who got their students involved. How did they do it? Can we use the same techniques today?

> John 4:10
> Jesus answered and said unto her, If thou knewest the gift of God, and who it is that saith to thee, Give me to drink, thou wouldest have asked of him, and he would have given thee living water.

CHAPTER 7

SOME BASIC TEACHING TECHNIQUES

Acts 17:22-23
Then Paul stood in the midst of Mars' hill, and said, Ye men of Athens, I perceive that in all things ye are very religious (ASV). For as I passed by. and beheld your devotions, I found an altar with this inscription, To THE UNKNOWN GOD. Whom therefore ye ignorantly worship, him declare I unto you.

We've just studied the need for getting involvement. Not only will the students be more motivated to learn when they find they are learning, but both the teacher and student can profit from the feedback that comes from involvement. Now let's see some simple ways of getting students involved and producing learning at the same time.

Sub-Group Activity Encourages Involvement

No matter how large or small the class is, it's always possible to break it into sub-groups. Adult classes can be broken into groups of 5-10 people, small classes can have only two people to a group. Several things are important here: first, the why. The reason for sub-group activity is just *that – activity*, which in turn produces more learning. Secondly, sub-group work helps increase the amount of *feedback* available to the students and the teacher. Another advantage to sub-group work is that it keeps students from getting lost in the crowd. They may not participate in large groups, but when the group is small, they have to contribute more. Finally, one big advantage is *the defining of the learning activity*. When the sub-groups are formed, they are given specific tasks. Often the tasks for learning aren't so clearly defined in large classes where the teacher does most or all of the talking. The sub-group work shouldn't consume all of the classtime. The small groups need not meet together for more than a few minutes – just long enough to reach some conclusions, work up a brief report, or prepare some material for presentation. The more groups there are, the less time that can be allotted, because there should be time for all the groups to report. The groups work better with less time, by the way, because the pressure of time reduces the amount left for side conversations.

Accountability is an important aspect of class activity, so all groups should somehow be responsible for each group's reporting. They can be told, "Come with the single most important point," or "Make out one question on each group's report," or "I'll ask somebody a question after each presentation." This way, everybody listens to all the reports, hence they should learn more.

Students Should Have Specific Goals

As we've said, one advantage of sub-group activity is that the goal or objective of the learning is fairly specific. This isn't always the case in our lecture efforts. When we make special efforts to get the students involved, we are more likely to think about just what it is we want the learner to be able to do at the end of the class period. Regardless of what method we use, however, we should know where we want the students to go.

This should be stated before class, and even told to the students. It might be a long range objective over several class periods, but shouldn't be too long to be realistic. For example, we might tell a group of teenagers that they will be able to quote twelve verses, give scripture references when they hear the quotation and be able to apply them to everyday problems and religious error. Obviously this is a project for several weeks, but by saying that this is the goal for three weeks' study, they know exactly what's expected of them. They also know how well they are doing week by week. Most important, *they will know when they have reached the goal.*

Questions And Answers Involve Students

When we think of ways to cause involvement, one of the first things we think of is a question and answer session. When used properly, this is a good method. If we're able to put the questions in good form and are able to get solid answers back, then we cover the material, cause involvement and both the teacher and the students get good, useable feedback. But questions sometimes are ambiguous and people hesitate to answer, not because they don't know the answer, but because they don't know the question! A few times like this and the teacher soon discovers that no one answers any questions, even the simple ones. This brings us to one big problem in the question and answer technique: it only involves one person at a time.

How can we get better use out of this technique? There are several ways, each with advantages and disadvantages. One obvious way is to call on a specific person, going to a different one with each question. This way the entire group is alert, waiting to see who will get the question (provided we ask the question *before* we specify who is to answer it), and can relate their answer with the one given. The drawback is that in older groups this can lead to embarrassment.

Some may not like to be put on the spot, some may not like to answer out in class, some may not be prepared and some may not understand the question. In any of these situations the teacher may do more harm than good by continuing to use the technique, unless he can find a way to overcome the difficulty.

One important point here: perhaps the worst possible use of the question and answer technique is to go down the row asking one question at a time, especially from a workbook of some kind. Each person knows well in advance which is going to be his question and he thinks about little else until his turn comes. After he has answered, he doesn't think about anything since his turn won't come for a long time.

Another way to build in accountability is to have some member of the class verify an answer. The teacher asks the question, someone answers, and the teacher-without saying the answer is right or wrong-asks, "How many agree with that?" By a show of hands those that think the answer is right verify it. Those that don't hold up their hands are fair game to be asked, "What do you think it is, then?" and point out someone specifically. After awhile the group learns to respond with conviction because accountability has been added! Of course, this can go on several more steps. When the person who disagrees gives his answer, the teacher still doesn't have to reveal the correct answer. He simply does the same thing again, "How many think *this* is right?" Now the two groups have an interest in finding out which one is right, and they are waiting with interest. The good teacher will have each defend his position until the answer is settled.

Competition Should Not Be Misused

This brings up the question of competition. There are those who say they are opposed to competition in Bible teaching, but perhaps that's because of the bad connotations given to the word. In reality, every time a question is asked and several excited young hands go up, each child eager to be the one to get to answer the question, competition has come into the classroom. Giving stars for attendance or memory verses is appealing to the element of competition.

So it's hard to say that all competition is bad. The important thing about competition, just as with playing games, acting out stories, cutting out pictures or pasting and coloring: the end is the important consideration. If competition, games, coloring or any of these things become an end in themselves, they are out of place in my teaching-learning situation.

Building accountability by groups or individuals by keeping track of how well each is doing is an excellent way of keeping interest and encouraging involvement. The process doesn't have to be complicated.

Just giving 10 points for right answers will start it off, and it's a matter of going on from there. The rule is *keep it simple, move fast and don't get lost in the process* itself. One way to keep from getting lost in the process is to start the scoring over as soon as one side or individual gets too far ahead of the rest. This can be done even within a class period or from week to week. Also, if one person or one group consistently gets ahead, mixing the groups helps maintain the interest of everyone.

Role Playing Interests Students

One of the most effective ways of getting realistic involvement in Bible study is through the process known as "role playing." This is more than just acting out a story; it involves having the person play the role of some person and make up the story as he goes along, trying to stay in character as he goes. For example, when studying about various religious beliefs, have one of the students play the role of someone who holds that belief. This way he will have to study and try to find ways of playing a convincing role. If prejudice is a part of it, he must have the same prejudice. If liberality is part of it, he must play that, and every argument must reflect that belief. This allows those observing or participating to see just what the position would have to be to be consistent. This is quite different from a debate in that that there is no set time schedule and each reacts as he thinks the role requires, whether it strengthens his argument or not. Oftentimes the teacher will require the students to switch roles half way through the discussion so that each will get the feel of the other side. Carrying the idea further, some teachers will have the class divide in half and while one person plays the role in each group, the discussion is stopped every few minutes while the role players get together with their respective groups and decide what to say next. The technique is very good at building interest and involvement, especially when it is difficult to get the group to see how other people feel and think. Being able to see someone applying what is being talked about makes the subject more easily acceptable.

What subjects lend themselves to role playing? Almost any "application" type lesson does. *Dealing with religious error* is very effectively taught by this method, from early teenage upward, even in adult classes. The teacher has to be bold enough to try it, but once he does, the group takes to it quite readily. Young adults and teenagers get especially excited about this technique because it has a way of making the subjects come alive for them. Seeing immediate application of the things they are studying always makes the study more meaningful. Another good application of the role playing technique is in studying application of *Christian principles* to everyday life. One of the students plays the role of the Christian and the teacher plays the part of someone with an arrogant attitude, or one who is discouraged, or someone who has turned away from the faith, or any other application that needs to be studied. Another application is *in personal* work study. The combinations are endless, depending only on the imagination of the teacher. The teacher can play the part of an indifferent neighbor, or a very devoted (but religiously wrong) individual, or an interested person who has a family problem, or a person who thinks everyone is right as long as they are sincere. Again, the possibilities are endless.

There are other applications to the role playing technique, but these will suffice to give the idea. There are several things that should be noted about the process, however. One thing is that while it is a good technique, it can be overdone. The most effective uses come when the teacher can drop into the role casually, make the points quickly, then stop the exercise and go on to the discussion of what happened. Since role playing gets to be enjoyable and even humorous sometimes, there is a tendency to let the process go on too long, even after the points are well understood by everyone.

Along this same line, the teacher should see to it that everyone takes the exercise seriously and should not let it get out of hand. This is why it's usually a good idea for the teacher to play one of the roles. Neither person has to be an actor, by the way. All he has to do is let himself "feel" the role a little. Sometimes giving a little information about the situation helps some. The teacher can even write out a few points for the person playing the other role so that he will get the feel of the character sooner. The important thing is for the people playing the roles not to change characters in the middle of the exercise. (This is one more reason for only letting the role playing go on for 2-3 minutes.)

Case Studies Motivate Students

Closely akin to role playing is the technique called "case study." In this process, the teacher makes up a little situation and lets the group come up with a solution to the problem. The case is usually a very basic one that presents some kind of dilemma. The group (preferably broken up into sub-groups) comes up with a solution but must substantiate it with scriptures. Often the solutions may be different, allowing the students to see that sometimes there are several solutions to some of the problems we run into. The important thing is for them to see that the only acceptable solutions are those that can be backed up with scripture. Here are some examples of cases that might be used in different circumstances and with different age groups:

Young Adults

Mary and Charles have only been married for a short time. They have no children. Charles isn't a member of the church, although he grew up in a fairly strong denominational family. Mary is strong, but has run into a problem. They have only one car and lately Charles has started to use it on Sunday morning to go fishing, leaving her without a ride to services several miles away. Charles's parents live next door to them and have offered to take her with them to their church anytime she wants to go. Charles has even said that he will stay home and go with her if she will go to the denomination where his parents go. "In fact," he says, "if you go with them a few times, I expect they'll even go with you when the meeting comes up next month at your church."

1. What would you do if you were Mary?
2. Give scriptures.

Teenagers

Debbie and Al are in second year of high school, and have dated a few times. Al is a member of the church, leads singing on Wednesday night and attends regularly. A couple of times Debbie has gone with him. Tonight they are double-dating with another couple, Bill and Sue, because Bill has his driver's license and can get the family car. Al doesn't know Bill too well, but Bill seems to be a nice guy. Bill has invited them to go on a cookout at one of the nearby state parks. When they get there, Al discovers that Bill has a case of beer in the trunk and the cookout is really just a beer party with a number of other couples all drinking. Debbie is just as surprised as Al, but thinks that he knew what it was going to be all the time. When he denies it, she says, "Well, what are you going to do now?"

1. What should Al do now?
2. What got him into this situation?

3. How could he avoid it next time?
4. Give scriptures.

Ten to Twelve Year Olds

Nancy has always tried to do what is right and has the reputation of being honest. The teachers all know they can trust her. There is a new girl in the school named Marie who sits behind Nancy. Marie and Nancy are becoming close friends and Nancy has been helping Marie with her math in the evenings since Marie is having a lot of trouble. Today in class they had a test, and while the teacher was out of the room, Marie leaned over and asked Nancy to move her hand so she could see one of Nancy's answers. Without thinking, Nancy did. After class, Marie thanked her in front of all the other girls. "That was really great!" she said. "That's really friendship. I won't forget it. If you ever need any help on a test, just whisper for help."

1. What is "real friendship"?
2. What is the difference between character and reputation?
3. What scriptures could be used to solve this problem?

As can be seen, the cases are simple, but straightforward. They aren't complicated or confused. Most important, they deal with everyday problems that can and do happen. By making scriptural application, the students will see that the Bible actually does apply to today's problems. Often these cases will last a whole study period, because the discussion can profitably include ways of seeing that these problems are avoided as well as solved. Also, the class can usually think up problems from their own lives that can be discussed. The beauty of this is that the students in the Bible class are making direct application *for themselves* of the Bible to the everyday problems they are faced with. Any teacher should be more than elated to have this happening in his class. There is no age limit, either. Adults get just as involved as do the young.

The *main* thing is to keep the cases simple, practical, realistic and aimed at a particular subject. Also, the discussion should always end with *scriptural answers, not just opinions.*

Play Acting Teaches Bible Stories

We've purposely made a difference between role playing and play acting. There is quite a difference between making up a case or having someone play a role with their own imagination being the guide, and acting out a story in the Bible. When we have the young people act out the lesson from some event in the Bible, we would like to have it as near to the Bible account as possible. The purpose of this type of technique is quite different from the ones we've been talking about previously in this chapter. One – acting out the Bible story – is designed to assist the student in remembering the Bible account, and needs to follow the story exactly. The others – making up cases or roles to play – depend upon the imagination to guide in *the application* of Bible truths. Each is equally effective when used for the right purpose.

One of the largest assets to be found in a class full of young children is an almost *unlimited imagination*. There are very few things that they cannot get excited about, and their minds are alert and waiting for a challenge to be used. Nothing fits this challenge like acting out the story they are studying. The teacher who can capture this imagination by letting them act out the things they are studying receives a bountiful reward.

Here again, the rule is to *keep it simple*. There is no need for elaborate props or costumes. A chair can be a camel, a boat, an army of people on horseback or anything else it is called. The trick is to let them use their imagination in naming these things. They enjoy acting out the same story, too, so it doesn't hurt to change the roles and let different ones go through the same story again. The main thing is to see that they get the point of the lesson, and that the words and actions come close to simulating the ones in the Bible story.

Testing Gives Feedback

In talking about teaching techniques, it is important to see where testing fits into the picture. Testing generally has a "bad name" as far as Bible study is concerned, but it can be used effectively to produce learning. The important thing is to get the purpose of the testing in the right perspective. The main purpose of testing is not to teach. Those who say that this is "another teaching tool" should be careful not to give the impression that teaching is the primary function of testing. The primary function of testing is simple enough – to give feedback to the teacher and the learner as *to how much learning has taken place*. It is sometimes used improperly as a threat to get students to study. It is used improperly to punish those who have not studied. It is best used as a means of letting both the teacher and the student know where success and failure lie.

Testing needn't be dreaded. It needn't even be written out and given like a schoolroom device. When we think of testing as just a feedback device, we see that any time we ask a general question in class, we are, in fact, "testing." Any time a student answers a question from a workbook, he is being tested If we can get our students to think along these same lines – and we can if our testing has no threatening elements in it – then they will not cringe when they are faced with a few questions on a piece of paper instead of asked orally. What is done with the results is more important than what the students make on the test. If both the students and teacher see that much has been learned, then each can be satisfied. If little has been accomplished, neither can feel very good. But the important thing is to see that correction is made in the teaching and learning process used so that the results will improve next time.

Individual Reports And Assignments Involve The Students

One age-old technique that has proven its worth many times, but often gets overlooked, is the process of having individuals in the class make reports on selected subjects. The assignments can be made in advance or they can be made right in class. The teacher can ask a student to look up something in a reference book at the building and make a report on it before the period is over. The teacher can assign someone (or several people) to look up material and report on it at the next meeting. This can be planned or it can come spontaneously. If someone asks, "What's the difference between the Pharisees and the Sadducees?" the alert teacher can see this as an opportunity to get some involvement. "Who'll look that up for next week and tell us what they find?" He can even ask someone specifically to take on the assignment. The good of this is that the subject to be discussed the next week is one that came from the students, so it is of interest to them. It also allows the teacher to go on with what he has planned without cutting off interest.

These reports work equally well with the teenagers. They have alert minds that can consume a lot of facts in a short time. If they aren't doing too well at studying, reports often will build their interest. Even giving them an assignment after class has begun will work very well. Give them ten minutes to report on part of the lesson; divide them into small teams and let them decide how the reporting will be done. They will move fast and efficiently and surprise us with what they can do when they know you are depending upon them. Here, again, is an excellent method for getting feedback to see how well the students are grasping a subject. They are teaching themselves, discovering the points for themselves, and certainly learning more as a result of the involvement.

There is actually very little difference between these reports and the "show and tell" the very young enjoy so much. We should mention this technique, however. It's a little different from the "acting" we discussed earlier. A good example would be where the teacher has told a story using a flannelboard, then lets each child have part of the story to tell, using the pieces of the paper making up the story. Each uses his piece of paper to tell his part of the story, then places it on the flannel The process can be repeated as many times as the teacher sees fit. It is important that the teacher not be concerned with whether or not the pieces of paper are straight or right side up. With their imagination, it doesn't matter to them. If they think it looks all right, it is all right!

Conclusion

Many times people will ask, "What's the best teaching technique to use?" That's a lot like asking a housewife, "What's the best cooking utensil to use?" The best technique to use is the one that works the best with the subject being taught, the students being taught and the ability of the person doing the teaching. There are some measures, however. The best techniques are those that get the most involvement, provide the teacher and the learner with the most and best feedback possible, and fit the time limits of the class period. The more the students are involved, the better the pacing will be for their individual learning. The more the teacher does, the more the pacing is set for the teaching instead of the learning. When the teacher does all the talking, time is constant and learning is the variable, since each student learns at a different pace, but the teacher is putting out the information at only one rate. As the students get more and more involved, the pace becomes more suited to their individual needs, and can even vary with each person participating. Now learning is becoming constant while time may vary from one student to the next.

DISCUSSION ACTIVITIES

1. Break the class into three sub-groups. Have group 1 list ways of getting involvement from students. Have group 2 list methods of getting accountability built into the exercises. Have group 3 list ways of getting feedback. Compare these findings when the sub-groups have finished. Notice the similarities in the methods. In the final

analysis, it's impossible to separate these three requirements – when we have an activity that gets feedback, it usually gives the student accountability for the learning, and it certainly takes involvement to have these things.

2. Again, break the group into sub-groups. Have each group set a specific learning objective for someone studying the 23rd Psalm. (What would you want them to know-or be able to do-at the end of the study?) Now compare the results. Are they measurable objectives?

3. Repeat the process for someone studying Acts 2. Compare the results. Is this the way that we usually study the Bible? What are the advantages of this method?

4. Now look at the results of the findings of both Questions 1 and 2. Group discussion - decide two things: how would we teach each of these to reach the objectives set and how would we find out if we had reached the results? Would feedback and involvement help in each case? Could we know if we had reached the results without feedback?

Acts 4:19-20

But Peter and John answered and said unto them, Whether it be right in the sight of God to hearken unto you more than unto God, judge ye. For we cannot but speak the things which we have seen and heard.

PART III

TEACHING BY AGES

CHAPTERS 8-13

CHAPTER 8

PRESCHOOL CLASSES

Matt. 19:14
But Jesus said, Suffer little children, and forbid them not, to come unto me, for of such is the kingdom of heaven.

Introduction

Here is the beginning-the first chance on a group basis-that we are able to teach the Bible to the very young. They come to us virtually ignorant of God, Christ, the Holy Spirit, love, sin, forgiveness and all the things they will someday have ideas and opinions on. We are the ones that help form those ideas. *Where they go from here depends a great deal on what they get here.*

Can They Learn?

One of the most serious mistakes new teachers make about the students of the preschool age is that their job is essentially one of "baby sitting," not teaching. They wrongly assume that no one at this young age can really learn very much, and certainly not *any concepts*, just facts. Another mistake is based on this wrong assumption: letting the inexperienced teacher have this class, since there is little harm done if the teacher doesn't do a good job. After all, it's hard to find someone who is even willing to "sit" with this age!

The answer to those who ask if this group can really learn is that only those teachers who have never taught the preschooler would ever make the assumption that they are little more than vegetables that have to be "baby sat" with. The teacher who has had even limited experience with this age knows full well that while the differences may be marked between students, they all can learn much and well. And they aren't limited just to facts, either. They can learn concepts of great import, as we will see shortly. Yes, they can learn.

What Can They Learn?

They can begin to put together some facts into concepts. They may tend to oversimplify, and may not get the concept in its fullest form, but nevertheless they can, even at two and three years old, think pretty big thoughts. The following true experience of a very good teenage teacher demonstrates the point: In an effort to get the two and three year olds conscious of the presence of God, she had told them several times not to' be too noisy because God was present. She admittedly wasn't sure how well she was getting the concept across, but continued to use the scheme. One incident proved to her that they really were getting the concept and believed it unquestionably. When one of the little girls dropped her paper from the table, she started to slide her chair back to get down and get it. The small child next to her turned to her almost in disgust and said, "Don't make that noise, just leave it there, God will get it for you."

Whether we like or dislike the way the concept was created isn't the point. The point is that the young children had gotten the concept that God was present and saw this in a very real sense. It is doubtful that many adults can gather up that much of a true belief in the actuality of God's presence every time we assemble. The unquestioned acceptance of God's presence is quite remarkable at any age, but not at all unexpected from preschoolers.

First Glimpses Are Important

Perhaps one mistake we make that leads us to doubt that these young ones can understand concepts is to fail to make proper distinction between understanding the concepts *in all their deepest meanings* and understanding them *in a very small but accurate* way.

For example, few of us would admit to understanding the fullest meaning of an all-powerful God. If we studied for a lifetime we would still be inadequate in our understanding. But this doesn't keep us from studying about God. Neither does it keep us from introducing the concept of a powerful force of love and power that sees and knows and cares and hears and can do anything and wants to help us. Again, this doesn't mean that they will understand everything, nor will they necessarily have a completely accurate understanding of what they have. But it's a start and it's better than just learning the *fact* that God is. And this is what we're suggesting: begin very early to teach concepts of the Bible, not just facts. Left with the facts, they will form their own concepts or forget the facts because they have nothing to pin them to.

At this age they are ready to learn the concept of sharing, for instance. Even though they are being taught these things at home, hopefully, they still need to learn them in the context of the Bible. How do they learn sharing? Obviously there are a number of ways right in the classroom that the subject of sharing with others can be taught. The important thing is to keep making the point that sharing is one of the ways of pleasing God. We extend this to their home activities, also. Constantly we relate their activities, sharing and pleasing God all together. In the process we discover we are teaching yet another concept: the fact and idea that pleasing God is something we need to do at home, at play, anywhere we are.

Further, we are showing that God's teachings are applicable to everyday life, not just something that we turn on occasionally to seem religious. This is an important concept that wanes early in life, so teaching it here is none too soon. The stronger we make the point the better off the student is. Or perhaps we should say, the stronger the student makes the point for us, the better off he is!

Another concept that can be taught early is the all powerfulness of God. It is a dynamic point and one that the young people will readily accept, since they already think that most adults fall in this category. We might build on the error of this thinking with them. They need to learn early that their parents are not faultless, but not in a detrimental way. We show that even though their parents are very good and strong and smart, they sometimes make mistakes, even find things they can't do. But not so with God. Let them think of some very hard things to do, things their parents probably couldn't do, and get them to saying, "God could do it." They don't end up thinking less of their parents; just more of God. We won't go on with concepts that can be taught at this age, but a good exercise for teachers to go through is to do some brainstorming on just what concepts can be taught at what ages. Be sure to have someone there who has taught the various ages, especially the preschoolers, because we are apt to attribute less to their capability than they actually have available to use.

Put The Senses To Work

At the very early preschool age, the students aren't very good at using words, but there is nothing wrong with their senses. They can hear, see, touch, smell and taste. Their absence of words doesn't mean they can't understand and learn by other means. This is one of the best places for good visuals the teacher will ever find. Appealing to the sense of sight makes for good teaching here because the student has a limited vocabulary. But there are other senses. There is the sense of hearing-meaning this is a great time to sing songs about stories in the Bible. They have an interesting ability to sing even before they can speak. They pick up sounds of the songs and imitate them, even though they may not always understand the meanings. By putting the sounds into their minds we are, in a way, storing them up until the student is able to perceive the true meanings. (Hopefully, at some date not too far off the teacher will fill in the meanings. It's sad when children six and seven years old can sing "Jesus Loves Me" but can't answer the question, "How do you know Jesus loves us?" The song has no real meaning to the youngsters.)

The other senses can easily come into play, too. This age is great for "hands on" teaching. Let them feel dolls that represent characters from the Bible. Let them feel the sand as they place sticks or buildings in a sandbox. "How would you like to walk for many, many miles in this if it was so hot you could barely stand to touch it? Christ walked in this so He could teach people about God." Let them place the pictures on the flannelboards, draw on the chalkboard (make marks, if that's all they can do), set models on the table, or anything else they can do to use their hands and imagination. If the teacher has a small statue of Buddha, let the students feel it, handle it, talk about it, while the teacher tells about people bowing down in front of idols. Incense can be bought in novelty shops and other places. Let the students smell the burning incense while the teacher tells about how it was used in the Bible or why we don't use it any more.

They Will Oversimplify

One of the beautiful things about the preschool age is that everything comes out simple for them. Things often fit into place and make sense to them that would leave older children confused and in doubt. It isn't that these students are smarter, it's just that they tend to oversimplify because of their lack of background. In the process of making everything fit into place they have a tendency to make things simpler than they really are. This means they are misunderstanding things sometimes. What does the teacher do? Probably the safest thing to do is nothing. Trying to unsimplify will only confuse them at this stage and not accomplish much towards explaining the complete meanings to them. This doesn't mean that they should be left with glaring error. It means that they may not understand where Jesus went when He went to heaven, and may think He went up into the sky somewhere. The important thing is to know that He left the grave, conquered death and gave us a chance to do the same thing, not so much that He is now in some place which we feel impelled to locate for the student. Let "Heaven" take care of the location, in other words, let him decide for himself where he wants to put heaven for the time being.

There are some dangers in the oversimplification, however, that we should worry about. They aren't able to distinguish fact from fantasy at this age. They may not be able to understand the difference between Mother Goose and Baby Moses. It isn't as important at this age that they understand the difference but the time is going to come soon when they need to make the distinction very clearly. The preschool teacher needs to prepare them for the time they separate the two worlds by constantly using expressions like, "When Jesus was a little boy just like you..." and "He had a mother and a father just like you do, and he loved them like you do..." They may be too young to understand many things but they aren't too young to begin to get the concept that the people in the Bible were real people and the events aren't just fairy stories. It isn't so much the teacher's job to destroy the myths of the nursery rhymes as it is to establish the realities of the Bible. A good foundation at this age will last a long time!

Attention Span Is Short

Anyone who has ever taught this young age knows how short the attention span is. The unfortunate teacher who has gone in thinking that all that is necessary is to pick an interesting story and then spend the next forty-five minutes telling that story learned a lot about the attention span of this age in a hurry. The unskilled teacher probably makes the mistakes of then spending a great deal of time in correcting the students, thinking that she has a very unruly group. The better arrangement is to keep them so busy they can't get rowdy. (There is an interesting phenomenon here that might teach us a lesson. We ought to be glad that this age gets rowdy when they get bored. As the age increases, the rowdiness tends to decrease. By the time they are seniors in high school, they have resorted to remaining inactive when the attention runs out. Now we don't have to deal with it. The same is true in teaching adult classes. Adults often hide in the class and never do anything, many times because they aren't involved or paying attention.

Here again, we tend to ignore this group, and let them go on not learning anything. At least the young people get some attention from us when their attention span runs out. That's more than we can say, usually, about the older people. In other words, be glad about the rowdy students – they're *telling us something*.)

Instead of spending our time correcting the students, we need to keep them as busy as possible. This means story telling for a short time, songs for awhile, games for awhile, hand and body activity for awhile, even moving around if possible, then more stories, songs, etc. The larger the class, the more important this becomes, because the more distractions there are. The unprepared teacher of this group is very much out of luck in keeping the group satisfied. She is doing a disservice to the children, too, if she isn't ready to deal with them on many levels of activity. This is no place to feel embarrassed about getting down on the floor, or being actively involved in storytelling. The good teacher gets just as excited as the students do.

Team Teaching Can Pay Off

Of all the places where team teaching pays off, it pays the most dividends with this age group. Team teaching is the process of having two teachers in the class at once, dividing up the activities as they choose to. The advantages are obvious:

two people using their imaginations instead of one, two people preparing the assignments; two people observing the group and making decisions as to the needs and problems, one person always observing while the other is busy teaching, one person available to take one of the students to the water fountain or restroom while the other teaches on, one person ready to step in with another activity when the other finishes or runs out of material, and many more.

At the preschool level all of these advantages can be used. We've already seen that the attention span is short and there needs to be a number of activities available to the students. Team teaching provides that opportunity quite well. By properly planning *ahead* of time, the two teachers can work very well together. One takes care of the storytelling, the other takes over with some songs. One plays games with them or acts out stories while the other tends to restroom duties or water fountain activities. One can hold the little ones in her lap to overcome anxieties on occasions, allowing the other to go on with the planned activities. All of this paces the class very well and allows one teacher to rest and get her breath while the other is carrying on the teaching. It's important that the teachers work well together and not have any inhibitions about "performing" in front of another adult.

Keep It Simple

We have already pointed out the limited vocabulary of this group and the oversimplification efforts on their part. Let's look at this further. The lessons should be kept simple, obviously. But there is more to it than that It isn't enough just to keep the story simple: the number of points to be remembered should also be limited. The same story told to older students would tend to have many more points to be remembered. For this group, the main points should be held to just one or two. We say to ourselves before the class begins, "If they could just remember one thing, what would I want it to be?" If we do this, then we should carry it a step further: we should see if they can *say that one thing*. It's not necessarily a good class just because everybody participated and sang and listened to the story. It's a successful class only if the students can remember – or say – the one or two things we wanted them to be able to say when we planned the class. The real measure of success, then, is whether or not that one main point was gotten across. Of course, if that point was a concept, then we don't just want them to tell us that "sharing is good." We want to know if they can apply this concept. "What are you going to do when there is only one piece of cake left and your friend from next door comes in while you're eating?" "When two or three of you are playing and there is only one tricycle, what are you going to do?" The answers to these questions will tell us a lot about how well we got the concept across.

We started talking about keeping it simple; let's see another side of this problem. Remember we said that the vocabulary is limited. This means that there is a limited meaning to certain words, too. The best way to point out how this becomes a problem is to relate another real incident.

A very good teacher with considerable experience was trying to get the group excited about the story of the good Samaritan. In her usual inventive way, she decided to let them really get into the story by playing it out. She came to class with enough bandages (strips of an old sheet) for each student in the class to play the part of the wounded man. She figured that all of them would want to play this part and she planned for each to lie down on a mat and have the others take care of the "poor man," even to helping him to the inn. All of this sounded very good in preparation, but it didn't work out very well, because of a vocabulary problem. She briefly told them the story, then told them they were to act it out. When she asked them, "Who wants to play the hurt man?" no one volunteered. Not only did they not volunteer, but even when she almost forced one to take the role, the others got into their roles very hesitantly and without any excitement. She suspected the problem, but knew for sure when a parent revealed that later in the week her child had said at the breakfast table (out of a clear sky), "I don't have to be the hurt man, do I, Mommy?" It became painfully clear to this very good teacher that her choice of the word "hurt" was wrong. They could not assign a value to hurt without the pain. Once they got the idea that playing the hurt man would be painful, there was little the teacher could do to dispel the idea, even if she had known for sure that this was the problem.

Make Lasting Impressions

There is a wonderful frankness about these students. They will say what they think, especially the older preschoolers. They often reveal things about their home and family life that shouldn't be broadcasted, perhaps, and the teacher shouldn't pry, of course. But the teacher can use this frankness to her advantage. We talked several times about getting feedback from the students about how they are thinking.

The frankness helps us to do this. The questions we mentioned earlier in this chapter to see if they have the concepts will work only for those students who are open in their speech. As we mentioned in the chapter on techniques, the more the individual says something the more likely he is to remember it. This is much more true than when we say it many times to them. For this reason, we should take advantage of their frankness to get them to discuss the applications of the lessons back home. We should remember we are making lasting impressions – first impressions, too – so we want them to be well organized and stated often. So we have them repeat and repeat. The next time they come into class, they repeat some more. Not long, complicated activities – just simply statements and applications. Go around the room, letting each participate. Let them say the words together. Let these first impressions be simple ones, important ones and ones that will stick in their minds.

Something as simple as "When in doubt, don't" can stick with them for the rest of their lives. The important thing to remember here is that the teacher shouldn't get lost in the one lesson period. She should realize she is framing a future faith. She should want to hear as much evidence as possible as to how this framing is taking place.

Furniture Arrangements Is Important

When it comes to furniture, there is no set way that works the best under all conditions. Different teachers prepare different kinds of activities, so require different kinds of room setups. Some teachers prefer not to have any furniture at all with the very young so they can get down on the floor with them and carry on the activities. This avoids the problem (so common to most) of moving, sliding, overturning chairs. As they reach the upper limits of the preschool age, they are learning to sit, and chairs and tables become an important part of the teaching activities. The chairs should be those that are easily, noiselessly and safely moved. All of the materials in the classroom should be at their eye level, *not the teacher's*. The chalkboard and flannelboard should be right down where they can use it. Pictures should be hung for the viewing of the students, not the teacher. If curling up on the floor is the best way to make the lesson come alive, then the furniture should allow for this kind of activity. One of the best assets to the room is carpeting on the floor, preferably the "indoor-outdoor" kind that is durable and cleanable. This cuts down the noise and lets the students get down on the floor without harm. Of course, getting down on the floor shouldn't be a playtime activity. It should be meaningful. As they get closer to school age, learning to sit quietly for a few moments is a valuable learning experience, and should be built into the lesson planning. But that isn't the primary function of the teacher nor the class period.

Conclusion

The preschool group is the vital one to the church. It is the future of the church. It is here that faiths, impressions, beliefs, concepts begin. The teacher is teaching for the future and should remember that with each concept that is developed. She might even say to herself, "If they don't get it now, will they get it at all?" They can learn concepts and we should try to teach them the proper concepts. We should also try to get a look at these concepts in the minds of the students by having them do a lot of talking and by making application. We want to see how they are thinking, not just tell them what we think. It takes a little practice, but with experience we can do it.

Finally, this age is a good age to break in the teenage teacher. Not because it doesn't take much knowledge to teach this age, but because it takes patience and energy and understanding. The young teenagers have a lot of this going for them when it comes to dealing with the preschooler. The ideal is to have the teenager working with an experienced teacher as an assistant, with both of them doing what they can do best. Teaching the very young isn't a job for the inexperienced alone. It isn't a babysitting job for the "willing but unimaginative." It is an important job for an enthusiastic Bible teacher who realizes the significance of what she's doing, and who wants to do it very well!

DISCUSSION ACTIVITIES

1. General Discussion: Drawing from the experience of the preschool teachers, make a list of "concepts" that preschool children begin to have a fairly good grasp of, such as "sharing," "caring," "God," etc. (With careful consideration, this list can become very long.)

2. In many congregations, the preschool class is taken by those who are new to the faith, the idea being that "after all, you don't have to know too much about the Bible to teach preschool ages." Discuss this approach, keeping in mind the list of concepts in Question 1.

3. Working in sub-groups, let each group "brainstorm" ways of teaching the story of the crucifixion of Christ, using as many senses as possible and getting the students as involved as possible. As each group reports, begin to collect a total of ideas. Discuss what would be the quality of teaching if every subject taught could be "brainstormed" like this.

4. Group discussion: List the various songs sung by the youngsters and decide what the message in each is. Now decide how many of the children really get the message from the songs. As a test of judgment on this, have the teachers of this age try it out on their class the next time she is with them. (Ask them how they know Jesus loves them. The answer should be, "Because the Bible tells me so," if they've been listening to the songs. Don't be surprised if they can't explain the meaning of the story about the wise man building the house on the rock.)

Acts 5:42
And daily in the temple, and in every house, they ceased not to teach and preach Jesus Christ.

CHAPTER 9

ELEMENTARY AGE

Phil. 1:14
And many of the brethren in the Lord, waxing confident by my bonds, are much more bold to speak the word without fear.

As children get into school and learn to read and associate with learning activities all day long, their lives change radically. Group associations replace single, family-type relationships. Whereas the children were learning to work as a group with some difficulty before this, they are now in their "natural habitat" when they are with other children. The Bible teacher, fortunately, doesn't have to train the students how to relate with the other students, nor to wait their turn to speak. While they may not abide by the rules, they really know that they must share time with the other people in the class. In other words, the teacher is free now to teach, not having the additional duty to help acclimate students to a group situation.

Advantages Of Teaching This Age

Good Active Minds. At this age they have good, active minds which are by and large uncomplicated with misinformation. True, they do have misconceptions, but these haven't been around long enough to become a permanent part of their "conceptual" lives. They still possess that tremendous ability to learn facts and memorize. They can learn new facts every week and not become mentally tired. They may get bored, but rarely ever get tired with mental fatigue. They are at an "impressionable" age that makes it easy for the teacher to get lasting messages to them, or rather to form lasting impressions because of things that they discover through teacher guidance.

At the early part of their elementary stages they aren't interested in the opposite sex and can function very well in mixed classes. Up until about the fifth grade they don't feel the strong urge to "show off" for the other sex. Another advantage of this age group is that they are generally anxious to please the teacher and will do whatever work is required to impress him or her.

Here again, there is that opportunity for the teacher to exert lasting impressions, not only on the child's lifestyle to come, but also on the child's study habits, which *means making learning a happy experience*. Unfortunately, children soon decide that Bible learning is supposed to be dull and boring, and in many ways, like doing penance. This group is in the age where that can be dispelled by good, innovative teaching techniques.

High Energy Levels. Their energy- of which there is much – can be challenged and channelled into constructive and productive efforts. They love to compete at any time during this age and will devote great time and energy to winning, just for the sake of winning. By the time they have reached the third grade, they are able to make simple reports from what they have read in the lessons. By the time they are in the sixth grade they can take a subject and with a little guidance, do some research for making reports. The topics need to be simple, and the resource material uncomplicated, but they will do the work if the opportunity is there. A further development of this idea allows them to make reports by working together as a team of two, even for competition. Caution should be taken in assigning reports, especially the first few times. Since it is a new experience for most of them, the early efforts should be met with much praise, and should not be criticized at all unless they have given erroneous information. For example, they could be given the assignment to find out where five of their friends attend services, and at least one thing that each friend believes about religion. They will have fun collecting and reporting the information. They will also be developing a habit of talking to others about religion in a non-threatening way. There's a good chance that they will be surprised at what they find out. If they are surprised to learn how little their friends know, use this as an opportunity to put the same question to them. How much would they (your students) know if they were asked the same question? A fun way of handling this – and one that is most effective – is to have them roleplay this in class.

Avoid embarrassing them, but let them try it. (This same process can be used to teach them how to interview their friends when the assignment is first made.) Another assignment for a report is to let them do some research as to where certain stories and events are found in the Bible. Give them three stories, say Samson, Noah and the stoning of Steven. Tell them they must find the book(s) and verses that tell this information.

The only restriction is that they cannot ask any one they must find it on their own. Such activities as this make a lasting impression on the students because they have to "discover" the information for themselves. As they get older and more Bible wise, the teacher can make it even more competitive by making the task more complex, but in the nature of the stories and the number of various places the events are related. This can be used in the classroom, by the way, and becomes an exciting learning event. Definite time limits should be put on the events and the class allowed to work in small groups to increase the involvement. If one group discovers the ease with which a concordance can be used, then all the groups should be allowed access to one.

Formative Leadership Qualities. This group begins to show some leadership qualities and these qualities should be allowed to express themselves. Here is where the small group assignments work well. As individuals show their leadership skills, the teacher takes advantage of it by rewarding the action with compliments and reinforcement.

There is a basic rule to follow in giving out assignments, by the way, that should always be adhered to: assume the individual has the ability to take the work and exercise the necessary leadership, unless the student has repeatedly demonstrated that he will not take the leadership role. It is most important that the teacher express complete confidence and also recognize any leadership that is exercised. The church is constantly looking for and needing good leaders. They do not happen – they are the result most often of repeated opportunities to grow and of being recognized for the efforts they make when they are young.

Disadvantages Of Teaching This Age

Now let's look at some disadvantages of teaching this age group. This is not to discourage teachers, because in every age bracket there are disadvantages as well as advantages. The disadvantages are no more than things for the teacher to watch for and use to his own advantage, if possible.

Most of the disadvantages are the reverse side of the advantages we listed. For example, we said that this age group has good, active minds, that they learn quickly and have little background as far as depth is concerned. The disadvantage comes when the teacher isn't prepared to cope with this type of student and settles down just to answer a few true and false questions and to discuss the lesson with the group. With the capability of this group, things can go downhill in a hurry. The class can become unruly, begin to play or not pay attention (not really limited to this group, but especially true of this age). The more unruly they get, the more the teacher may fuss and lecture, driving the activity further downhill. The class becomes a contest between the students and the teacher, and *the students* will always win in such a contest. The teacher will control the class, but little or no learning will take place. The students win from the standpoint of thwarting the teacher's teaching efforts, but of course, everyone loses in the process!

This disadvantage can quickly become an advantage when the teacher puts the time and effort into preparing for this kind of student. Of all ages to which lack of preparation by the teacher will do the most damage, no age will suffer more than this one. It isn't possible to keep energetic, active and enthusiastic minds meaningfully busy without plenty of preparation! It is a constant challenge to the teacher to come up with ways of utilizing all of this potential.

"Permanent" Damage. Another serious consideration with this age is their impressionable state. The teacher who doesn't realize that each class period is a chance to have the students

form lasting concepts may leave the impression that learning isn't really much fun. They may decide that Bible classes are all taught by dull, serious, unimaginative and uninteresting individuals. Such an impression, formed at this impressionable age, will be hard for another teacher to overcome later on. One has only to look around at adult classes and wonder how many of the students in these classes got the idea that Bible classes aren't supposed to be meaningful-just something you're supposed to attend every time they are held. This may also account for the lack of studying done at the adult age and at the critical teenage level.

The energy that these students have can prove a disadvantage in the hands of the wrong teacher. As we have said, if the teacher gets so interested in maintaining discipline (or keeping the class quiet) then the energy is going to fall into disuse or misuse. The worst thing that can happen to this age is for the teacher to appear to interpret their youthful energy as intentions of disinterest or disrespect for the Bible or the teacher. The teacher that clamps down is probably setting a stage for the teenager that evolves from this student. The next teacher will wonder why he has a sullen, disinterested, seemingly bored student. He may wonder why the teenager doesn't get excited about learning in the Bible class or why he doesn't voluntarily become involved in discussion. He may never know that the real cause is the way he learned about using his energy back in the early classes.

"Easy To Teach" Disadvantage. Because this age group can learn so well and handle material above what is usually given to them, they often lull the teacher into thinking a good job is being done. While it isn't wrong to say that a good job is being done any time someone learns about the Bible, it is a shame if the students haven't been challenged up to their abilities. If the class has the ability to do reports, to do research, to speak on its feet, to work successfully in small groups, to talk to those friends who are unfamiliar with the church, to learn at a rapid rate, to memorize – if all these abilities abound, and the teacher merely scrapes the surface, then an injustice has been committed against the student!

It would be wrong to assume that everything that has been said is true only for this age group. Good and bad teaching is pretty well the same for any age. Also, it would be wrong to lump all students in elementary ages into one category. Since we will discuss the early teenagers in the next chapter, though, this chapter deals with those children who have learned to read up to about the sixth grade. In the first three grades they react about the same to many learning situations. They are more dependent upon the teacher, they have less of the ability to comprehend deeper concepts, so are still having to learn the facts that someday will support the concepts they will form. They are more willing to accept learning for learning's sake and have less need to know exactly why they are learning something. They can memorize, but are unable (or unwilling) to spend long amounts of time memorizing lengthy passages. It can be done, but there will be a better time for it. Later they can make a direct application and still have the quickness of this age in their mental gymnastics.

The upper end of the spectrum – the fourth through the sixth grades – are the ones who can do more on their own and take on more complex assignments. The upper ages are able to work together and are less dependent on the teacher to guide them. At this age, too, it is even more important that they be kept busy, for they are beginning to reach the age when the opposite sex presents the challenge for attention. The teacher will have to begin to move the class period faster in order to use all the available energy. Even then, things will have to be watched to see that some do not devote an overdue amount of their time to impressing the others The task is a fun one, though, for the teacher, he can even use this to his advantage by having the boys compete with the girls in the various assignments. As we have said before, however, the teacher should be careful about using discipline at this age. The more pressure that is applied, the more the bubble is blown up, so that they will eventually explode and frustrate the teacher even more. This doesn't mean that discipline shouldn't be used, it means that discipline will become a fulltime job if that's all that's done to curb the energy and interest in the opposite sex. Ideally, the teacher should find ways to let this energy and interest in impressing others work for learning, rather than against it. This spells activity and even a certain degree of chaos. The teacher should remember that he can get things quiet any time he wants it. It's just that he *shouldn't* want it *all the time!*

Conclusion

The elementary age – from the beginning of reading to about the sixth grade – is the time when lasting concepts and habits of learning are being formed. In many ways it's like taking a brand new canvas and putting the first lines of a new painting on it. While this doesn't say that many lasting concepts haven't already been formed, it says that they are still malleable at this age and can be molded easily by the teacher. There aren't many Bible facts available from previous learning; only those basic stories they learned. They haven't used the Bible as a reference book yet and are beginning the learning process now. They are impressionable. They still look to the teacher with a little awe and a lot of respect. They expect the teacher to help them. Because of their energy and learning ability, a good, innovative, resourceful teacher will have the time of his or her life. An unenergetic, overly serious teacher may find the challenge too much for himself, and perhaps too much for the students to take, too. The ideal is for the teacher to allow them to devote all of their time and energy towards learning. It can be done. It's difficult, but a wonder to behold when it happens. In the years to come, the teacher who has been successful with this group will have perhaps more to show that has helped the church grow spiritually than anyone else among the teachers of any age group.

DISCUSSION ACTIVITIES

1. Make a list of the advantages in teaching this age of children, as given in this chapter. See if the group has any additional items to list. Now consider each of these as a group and see what there is about the advantage that the teacher can use to promote interest and learning in the classroom.

2. Repeat the process from Question 1, except this time list the disadvantages. As these are discussed, see how the teacher can take the disadvantage and turn it to his or her favor. (See how the disadvantage can work for the teacher instead of against him.)

3. Some teachers think teaching discipline at this age is the important role of the teacher, and they think of discipline as "keeping the children quiet all the time." When one walks by their classroom, sure enough, the teacher is talking and the students are being very quiet. In sub-groups, discuss this philosophy. Discipline can be defined differently than these teachers are defining it-what other ways can discipline be displayed? What else besides discipline might be showing in these classrooms, where no discussion is taking place?

4. Sub-group activity: Have each sub-group brainstorm ways of using up some of *the physical* energy of these children. The projects or exercises should be those that produce learning and that can be done in the classroom-without making so much noise that the other classes are disturbed. Report and discuss with the entire class.

5. Sub-group activity: Have the small groups research ways of getting the students *mentally* involved with reports and projects *in the class.* Report the finding to the entire class and discuss.

Acts 11:19-20

Now they which were scattered abroad upon the persecution that arose about Stephen travelled as far as Phenice, and Cyprus, and Antioch, preaching the word to none but unto the Jews only. And some of them were men of Cyprus and Cyrene, which, when they were come to Antioch, spake unto the Grecians, preaching the Lord Jesus.

CHAPTER 10

EARLY TEENAGERS

Acts 11:26
And when he had found him, he brought him unto Antioch. And it came to pass, that a whole year they assembled themselves with the church, and taught much people. And the disciples were called Christians first in Antioch.

Introduction

It may not be necessary to separate this age group from the previous chapter and the one to follow, but there is actually a definite difference between these children and the others. In a way, it's the frustration years before high school but after elementary age. It's the "not-belonging" years – the "sub-freshmen" age – the junior high days of not quite belonging. As far as the church is concerned, it's the vital years, the time when decisions are made that will determine what they will be doing just a few years from now. Those that think teenagers are lost as teenagers are wrong, teenagers start to be lost from the church activities *before* they get to be teenagers. Often they are lost just before it when they are on the threshold, not quite in, but already removed from the simplicity of childhood.

Bible teachers need to realize this and take advantage of the knowledge. A good rule to remember is: whenever you're in doubt as to how to treat this age, it's always best to treat them as older, not younger than they are. Since we watch them grow, it's hard for us to see the subtle differences that take place as they grow and change. For example, they are beginning to feel sophisticated, although their actions are still often that of unsophisticated children. They may tend to cut up in class, but resent being treated as the children they are acting like. How can all of this knowledge help the teacher? The teacher can be just as subtle by letting them do the things they liked to do as children, but make them think they are doing things a little more sophisticated. In this chapter we'll notice some of these things.

Use The Sophistication

One phase of sophistication that can be used in favor of the teaching of this age is the ability and desire to show some leadership. Asking one of the young men to serve as a leader of his group will find him taking the job very seriously, although the rest of the group may show little more than tolerance for him. They will, however, go along with him and let him be the leader, if for no other reason than to see that "their side" makes a good showing. The leadership roles should be spread around from week to week, of course, or the whole thing will become ineffective. One week the class can be broken down into sub-groups with a set of leaders who are responsible for the assignments, and with the responsibility of delegating how the assignments will be carried out. A small amount of classtime should be allotted for this organization. The assignments should not be too cumbersome or lengthy, and the expected outcome fairly simple. It may be no more than a section of the lesson for which each subgroup is to bring in one scripture apiece or one example from real life. It could be a challenge to see which group can bring the most scriptures or the most examples. Taking advantage of the "child side" of this age that still loves to compete, scores can be kept. For further accountability, each group should be responsible for checking the scriptures or examples of the other groups. This way they aren't left idle while the others are reporting. (By the way, this is a prime rule for any kind of class reporting at any age: *the rest of the class should always be accountable for what goes on during the reports.*)

Lecturing Is Out

This early age group has a characteristic of the later teens: they won't get much out of a prolonged lecture. The only difference is that the later teens will sit back and be bored while this age is still capable of being quite rowdy! They are smart enough at this age to bait the teacher a little, but not as much as they will in a few years. Often the mistake is made of putting a very sincere man in as the teacher who thinks this is the age to be sure they know all about their responsibility in many areas. While any age is the age to learn about responsibility, this surely isn't the *age to tell* them about it. They have too much life to sit idle while someone lectures to them, no matter how sincere the teacher is. If the teacher is really sincere about wanting them to learn their responsibilities, he will see that they get as *involved as possible* in every class meeting. The key to learning at this age (and most other ages) is to have them tell the teacher, rather than the teacher tell them. The teacher provides the settings for them and they draw their own conclusions – almost always right! The teacher needs only to provide a little correction and encouragement every once in a while to keep things moving along very well. Remember, while this age has begun to gain some sophistication they still have a refreshing degree of sincerity and desire for approval by their teacher.

Competition Still Works

As we have said before, most any age likes competition, and none like it any better than the age we're talking about here. They can get just as excited about trying to outscore someone else as the age group before them and have the capability of doing a great deal of work to achieve this end. As always, this group doesn't need a complicated system of scoring and an elaborate game to play. All they need is how many points they will get for a certain achievement and what the achievement is. The advantage to the use of competition at this age is that the *assignment* can be more complicated than just asking simple questions for which a few points are given.

In fact, in many ways, this age group has the ideal characteristics for the perfect class. They can read and understand what they read. They can get excited about competing and still concentrate on the subject they are studying. They have enough background to form many correct conclusions on their own. They still have respect for the teacher and pride in pleasing him. They will still do a reasonable amount of homework and will bring books and Bibles to class with them as a matter of course (if they are given the opportunity to get into the habit by getting points for bringing them!) They have the energy to put in a fast half hour or forty- five minutes in class and "run" all the way. They have enough leadership and followship to take an assignment and work in small groups without too much wasted motion (provided the assignment is clear and challenging).

They have the ability to express themselves and give teacher feedback as to what they think and what they have learned. While they are a little young to do much effective role playing where they have to do much thinking in the roles, they can take a simple case study and make a lot of good sense out of it. Most any teacher would and should be happy to have a class with this kind of ability. If a teacher has a group this age and is having trouble with it, he might ask himself if he's making the best use of all their talents!

Case Studies Are Effective Now

This age is the first one that can make consistent use of the case study method of teaching. The cases should be simple, deal with everyday life and lead to a specific Bible principle. For example, take the following situation.

Bobby Faces A Decision

Bobby has the reputation for doing well in school. He gets his homework and studies for the tests. While he doesn't always get the highest marks in school, he is usually up close to the top. Mike, a new boy in school, has had some trouble with his math and Bobby has tried to help him. Even so, Mike is still about to fail the math course. Today is test day and just as they are about to go into class, Mikes says to Bobby: "Hey, Bob, you think you're *ready* for this test?"

"As ready as I'll ever be, I guess." Bobby replied.

"Boy, I wish I were. I think I'm about to fail. I wish I were as smart as you are." Mike said, hanging his head.

"Aw, I'm not all that smart. Maybe you'll do all right. I hope so, anyway." Bobby said, trying to encourage Mike.

"I hope so, too, but I doubt it. Hey, I tell you what!" Mike said suddenly.

"What?"

"Since we sit beside each other, if I have any trouble, I'll slip you a note on which problems I need the answer."

Bobby hesitated a moment, then replied, "I'd like to, Mike, but I don't believe in cheating."

"Oh, you wouldn't be cheating. You'd already have the answer; just giving it to me wouldn't be cheating on your part."

"Well, I never thought about it like that..."

With just this much of a case, the teacher can get at least two or three good lessons, including cheating, choosing companions, having convictions, and protecting a good reputation. Any of these lessons has plenty of Bible settings and the scriptures are plenteous. An *additional* advantage to the case is that if the teacher assigns the task of coming up with scriptures to the students as an out of class activity, the students have a chance to talk to their parents about an important subject – one that might not come up in everyday conversation. Such cases as this should be simple, easy to believe, something that happens frequently, and something that makes a good, solid point with the students. It should be written at their level or slightly higher, and should use *everyday* language, but not too much "mod" language. Most important of all, the cases should *lead* to the conclusion, not *preach* to it. The conclusions reached should be those of the student, not the teacher. If the students are doing their jobs well – and with good cases they will – they shouldn't find it too difficult to reach all the correct decisions and summarize the important points while the teacher sits back and listens. Again: it's very important that the students reach the conclusions on their own, and state them in their own words. This way they will have much more commitment to the ideas discovered. Somehow, it just doesn't mean nearly as much when the teacher tells them what it is they were supposed to get out of the lesson!

Separate The Boys And Girls

The age we are talking about here is a good time to separate boys and girls into different classes, with effective men teaching the boys' classes, and good women teachers taking over the girls' classes. The purpose here is not so much because of the material being covered, but because of two other things.

First, this is the age when the boys and girls find it virtually impossible to resist trying to impress each other. Together they are a different class than when they are separate. Every answer is given to see its effect on the other people in the class. Wrong answers are laughed at and boys who would otherwise be quiet and mannerly find themselves becoming "cute" and eager for attention. The same is true for the girls. This isn't so much a discipline problem as it is a learning problem. Separation is almost sure to increase learning.

Secondly, this is a good time for the boys and girls to begin to take some leadership roles. They need to be on their feet making talks and reports. They will be much less self-conscious when the groups are in different classes. The girls can take more active parts, too, and begin to do some practice leading towards their eventual teaching roles.

When the boys and girls are separated, and cases are used as discussed earlier, the girls should have cases tailored to their own needs, using stories that talk about things they are interested in.

Conclusion

This is an exciting age to teach. Because of their natural eagerness to learn, we should be careful not to kill their interest by not giving them the best teaching available. They are at a critical age. They are going to make some decisions here that will go with them for the rest of their lives. It is here that they will make the decisions that may decide the future of the church where they attend, for here are the active young men and women of the next few years. With good teaching they will be a great asset. With poor teaching, they may not even be around.

DISCUSSION ACTIVITIES

1. This chapter mentioned that this is the "not-belonging" age group. Break into sub-groups and have each group brainstorm ways of making this group feel wanted, both in the congregation and in the classes. Be sure to include both boys and girls in your discussion. List these suggestions on the board and discuss.

2. As a group, look at the items on the board and see how many are now being used. For those that aren't, see what it would take to get them implemented.

3. As a group, make a list of the things a person at this age should know, assuming he or she had been attending Bible classes for most of his life. This should include such things as people he should know, lists of things he should have memorized, scriptures he should know, etc. Record this on the board and try to get unanimous agreement on the items. Now decide how many of the young people in this congregation really know these things.

4. Pass out pieces of blank paper and have each member start to take a test on the things listed on the board from Question 3. They don't have to sign their names, but the papers should be handed in or discussed. How much better are we than the young people?

5. This chapter has a case study – a story about Bobby facing a problem. Break into sub-groups and have each group make up a story that might be used for study at this age. Give each group a different topic, such as drinking, smoking, stealing, respect for civil authority, drugs, dirty

pictures and stories, and other subjects that are pertinent to this age group.

Acts 13:5
And when they were at Salamis, they preached the word of God in the synagogues of the Jews; and they had also John to their minister.

CHAPTER 11

TEENAGERS

2 Tim. 3:14-15
But continue thou in the things which thou hast
learned and hast been assured of, knowing of whom
thou hast learned them, And that from a child thou
hast known the holy Scriptures, which are able to
make thee wise unto salvation through faith which
is in Christ Jesus.

Introduction

Many words have been used to describe the teenager, all of
them accurate and incorrect at the same time. To try to say that
a teenager is a certain way or that there is a stereotype of the
present day teenager, is like saying that a tree is always a
certain way in looks. Just as a tree has seasons and looks
differently from one month to the next, so does the teenager.
Teenagers come in all sizes and shapes, not just physically, but
psychologically as well. To say that they are all bored in class
is as wrong as to say they are all excited about learning. To say
they all respond to certain activities is as wrong as to say they
respond to nothing.

The teenager is in the age of suspension – hanging
between childhood and adulthood. To the average adult, the
teenager is still small in his actions – while to the child, the
teenager represents the top of the ladder, big in every way. In
class we tend to treat them as children and expect them to act
like adults. In many ways, we are at a standoff with them:

"You act like an adult and I'll treat you like one," while they say to us, "You treat me like an adult and I'll act like one!" There is an ambivalence here that makes it possible for the teenager to be smart enough to do the work, at the same time smart enough to get out of it if that's what he wants to do.

Is It Hopeless?

All of this begins to sound like there is nothing we can do to be successful, which is obviously *a very wrong conclusion.* Just because the student is complex doesn't mean that there is no hope of success. Just because the job is challenging isn't reason for us to give up on the challenge. The truth is, for those who have taught this age group, the challenge is not equal to the immense satisfaction to be obtained from doing a good job. The rewards far exceed anything in the way of a problem that might exist. What we'll do here is to look at the things that most teenagers do have in common and see how we can apply this information.

First, however, let's look at some things about the learning pattern of this age group. If we think of learning as an extension of wherever we are already, we recognize that the teenager is at a point pretty far down the line of learning, if he or she has been doing any learning at all during the last several years of Bible study. (While we often find that this age is woefully weak in actual knowledge, they aren't too different from many adults with even longer histories of studying the Bible.) More important, this age is beginning to form some fairly rigid codes of conduct and attitudes toward behavior. Once these thought patterns are established, changing them becomes quite different from establishing them in the first place. The near-frightening thing is that they will form these attitudes *regardless of whether they are in class or not.* They will develop some kind of attitude towards the church, towards morality, towards their own religious place in life. They have a void and will fill it one way or the other. Their parents will help. Their public school teachers will help. Their peers will have a great influence on them. The Bible teacher must not only recognize the importance of the task of finishing out whatever void is left from early childhood, but also should know the competition. We certainly make a grave mistake if we assume they already accept all the principles we hold fast to, or if we go the other extreme and assume that they have only that information and only those attitudes that we are stressing.

Perhaps another mistake we make is to assume that the teenager has a logical pattern already developed and that our job is to add to it, fitting the pieces into a rational set of attitudes and ideas. The problem of the teenager is that he or she has had to operate in a world that expects reasonable and rational behavior and thoughts, but without the benefit of all the background and understanding that makes the behavior and thoughts come out all right. There are still big gaps and unanswered questions. Unfortunately, the teenager may not even know that these gaps exist. For a little while in their lives, things seemed very simple to them. They had, in fact, oversimplified life and its challenges. But now, things are starting to fall apart, not being as simple and straightforward as before. Depending on how much of this world has collapsed around them will be their ability to seem rational. For those areas where they think they have the answers, they will at least react *consistently*, if not completely reasonable. As they begin to discover that life itself is full of inconsistencies, they are less able to react the same way every time. It is here that the Bible teacher can have the most influence! The teacher provides the answers, the reason, the consistency that others haven't been able to provide.

Meet Their Needs

The best response from teenagers comes when the teacher is meeting their needs, dealing with subjects that they are interested in, handling problems they are confronting every day. This isn't always easy. Different towns and even different schools within the town may have entirely different problems for the teenager Christian. In one school or town, drugs – alcohol, smoking, strong drugs – may be the everyday problem, faced by all the children at every turn. In another location, drugs may never have been a problem at all. The same is true with sexual freedom as a problem. Different patterns develop in different locations and in different crowds within a school or group. It boils down to what the "in" thing is, "What are they all doing?" may be the things that the teenagers are the most concerned about. It is on these things the teacher can expect to get the most attention.

This doesn't say that we can no longer talk about the Bible. Now is the time to talk very much about the Bible and its application to everyday life. One of the gaps that must be filled for the teenager is the one that bridges the mysteries of the Bible and Bible subjects with the realities of everyday life. It is now, more than any other time in his life, that the student is searching to see if the Bible really holds the answers to such important subjects as: Whom do I date? What do I do on the date? How do I meet the temptations of the crowd? How do I work out the differences with my parents and family? How do I get to be independent and still keep a respectable relationship with those in authority? It is at this age they must decide that studying the Bible will solve the immediate problems of life. The skillful teacher makes the transition from just learning facts from the Bible to application of the Bible a smooth one for the teenager.

So the teacher's job in the teenagers' class is to provide an opportunity to preserve the security of the Bible teachings as it is molded into the real world. This is done by taking the simple position that everyday problems of today aren't any different in concept or complexity than they were thousands of years ago. The simple truth of the matter is that if people and/ or problems have changed that much then the Bible is a pretty useless piece of literature! What good are the laws of God or the commandments that tell us what to do from day to day, if the temptations, relationships and anxieties are all changed from the time God gave the information to us? *We have to face this ourselves* and come up with the strong conviction that the lust of the flesh, the lust of the eye and the vainglory of life was the same for Adam and Eve, David, Timothy and Paul, and is the same for John and Mary Doe. If we find ourselves saying that "today's youth face problems never before faced by young people," then *we'd better get out of the classroom.* At least the girls don't have to face the decision of whether or not to join their peers in giving themselves one day a year to the temple of Aphrodite as prostitute priestess, and the boys don't have to show their wealth and success by beginning to collect their concubines or explaining to their friends why they aren't going up to the temple to participate in the religious rites with the priestesses. Not only must we come to these conclusions ourselves before we go into the class, we must determine that our basic philosophy is going to be to convince the teenagers to find the answers to their problems in the pages of God's

Book, not in the opinions of their fellow teenagers, their school teachers nor even from their teachers of the Bible. The answers must be those that are found in the Bible so that when they no longer have their friends or teacher around, they are comfortable finding the answers in the Bible.

They Will Work Hard

The one complaint most often heard about teaching teenagers is the inability to get them to work at learning. The answer to this problem is nearly always the same: they really haven't been given the *responsibility* for the learning! From hour to hour in their public school life they are expected to be alert, study, give account for their activities, and generally handle difficult subjects with competence.

There's no reason why they can't build to that same competence in the Bible class. This says that we must give them something specific to learn, and they must know that they are expected to learn it – then we must let them learn it and *know they have learned it*. We simply find a way to let them take over the learning responsibility with our guidance. It isn't so hard to do, once we put our minds to it. (We should understand, of course, that they are usually smart enough to avoid taking the responsibility from us, if we aren't careful.)

There is something else to be remembered about this age group. Even in all of their sophistication, they still have a good deal of "child" left in them. This means they enjoy a competitive situation, they enjoy winning, they can still get excited and show it – providing the circumstances are right for it. It's up to the teacher to provide this circumstance. It has been said-correctly-that the only difference between playing games with elementary ages and teenagers is that you have to give points in the thousands instead of in the hundreds. The competition can be a lot more complicated, and the goal a little further down the road than with the younger folks. The teenagers can go a whole class period for one win or lose situation, whereas the younger ages needed more reinforcement than that. This works well for the teacher, because he can now give them a research project at the beginning of the period to be reported on halfway through the period, with the other groups being responsible for the content of all the reports. A brief test can be given at the end of the period, and it is on this the final score is made. This will keep their interest for the whole period, and provide for a healthy learning experience. There doesn't have to be any competition, of course, and many groups work well without this added motivation. The real incentive is the giving of concrete responsibility for the learning and then holding them accountable for what they have done. This means they work in small groups, a done if necessary, and approach the assignment any way they wish. If they are working up a debate, they work on it with whatever research material we can provide, but organize the material as best suits them.

Steps To Success

The obvious question now, is, What do I do as a teacher of the teenagers? One of the first things is to determine that no matter what happens, I will resist treating them like children until the very last effort has been expended to treat them as adults! But I won't have to keep telling myself this; I will accept it as a conviction and learn to react naturally, not by forcing myself. I will think like an adult, too, not like a parent, nor a preacher, nor an elder in the sense of thinking that the slightest deviation must be met with an immediate "straightening out" on the subject. I will explore *with* them. I will admit that some answers aren't cut and dried at least as far as a code of behavior is concerned. I will admit that it sometimes makes a weak argument to say that the best reason for not doing something is that it *just doesn't look right*. I will get them to try to come up with that conclusion, however, not force it ON them.

Next, I will try to find subjects they are interested in studying. I won't force them to go through a long, detailed study of the history of the Bible, when they are most concerned with how they can fit the Bible into their everyday lives. I won't force them to go through meaningless blanks and true- false questions, when they are really interested in how they can influence their friends and dates in the church. I will devote a great deal of energy to preparing exercises that are interesting and that involve the students to a very high degree. I won't expect to hold their interest for very long with my lecturing – I will keep their interest by keeping them busy. The work we do in class will be team work as far as possible. They will work in pairs; they will work on reports in small groups, organizing in any way they want to. The time limits will be held down. They will be forced to accomplish their work in short study periods, so that all energy will be devoted to the task. As their maturity grows, they will be given more mature assignments. They will work towards learning things that can be used in substituting in teaching roles for the younger classes. They will even work up special lessons to be presented to the younger groups on such subjects as simple approaches to proving the Bible is the word of God, and how to make decisions in school that will make us better respected as individuals. They will be allowed certain periods to discuss anything they want to, providing they can get the group to agree on the subject and can show that it is a Bible subject.

Finally, we will try to move these young people into responsible jobs in the work of the congregation. They will substitute teach, or take on assignments fulltime. The young men will learn to make talks, and as soon as they can, they will go before the congregation and present the talks. If possible, they will make these talks in times when there is an actual need: the adult Bible teacher is away or the preacher is absent. (They will be filling a need, not just "showing off.") The same is true of song leading. The young girls will not be forgotten, either. They, too, will have responsible jobs to do in the teaching work and in the caring for the communion trays and for making suggestions on ways of interesting the younger girls in learning to be elders' wives and preachers' wives and Christian mothers.

Conclusion

All of this says that these young men and women will be treated like the responsible people they must be in a very short time if the church is to survive in the manner we want it to survive. They are our leaders in the near future. We must start to let them take on some of the leadership under careful supervision!

DISCUSSION ACTIVITIES

1. As a total group, brainstorm a list of subjects that teenagers should be studying at their age. Be specific, and get group consensus. Think of ages from 15 to 18, rather than from 13 to 19. Get a group agreement as to the reason for studying each of these subjects.

2. Looking at the list from Question 1, decide what the young people this age would say to studying these subjects. Decide what they would have listed if they had made up the list themselves. (Hint: experience has shown that their list would look very much like this one if it includes such things as how to face the everyday problems of the world around them.)

3. Now look one more time at the list from Question 1 and compare this to what the people in this congregation are now studying. See how many in the group actually know what the young people are studying, excluding their teachers.

4. Just as in the last chapter, break into sub-groups and find ways that the young people this age can be made to feel a

part of the congregation. This must include more than just making a talk on Wednesday night or leading a song or prayer now and then – it must be a meaningful, *needed* activity.

5. Looking at the list from Question 4, which has been recorded on the board, decide which of these are now being used and which ones could be used with little or no effort. Make plans to see that they are implemented!

Acts 14:1

And it came to pass in Iconium, that they went both together into the synagogue of the Jews, and so spake, that a great multitude both of the Jews and also of the Greeks believed.

CHAPTER 12

THE ADULT CLASS

Heb. 5:12a
For when for the time ye ought to be teachers, ye have need that one teach you again which be the first principles of the oracles of God...

Introduction

This is sometimes thought of as the most difficult class of all to teach, and often the one that's the hardest to get people to teach. But with a little observation, we can see that in many ways this should be one of the easiest classes to teach. We'll look at some of the advantages of teaching this group. We will also see that there are some disadvantages as well, and many justifiable reasons why we often see people avoiding teaching this group. There are some things we can do that will make the job easier, however, and we'll examine those in this chapter.

What Does The Class Look Like?

Many who try to avoid this group say that they don't have the experience to teach it, since there is already a large amount of Bible knowledge in the group. The implication is that those who teach should always know more about every subject than any person in the class. This is nearly impossible and fails as an excuse when put to the test. (All of us recognize, of course, that it is desirable for the teacher, especially in the adult class, to have sufficient knowledge to lead an intelligent discussion on the subject at hand, and even be able to handle questions that are somewhat off the subject. But one of the real attributes of a good teacher is the ability to use the knowledge of those in the class. With this as a tool, the teacher can allow more digression from the subject knowing he will have help from the knowledgeable people in the group.) But not only is there usually a great deal of knowledge in the class, there is an unequal amount of participation. In fact, many adult classes can be characterized as not having any participation at all. So the teacher sees a group in front of him that may have the answers to the questions he is asking, but who probably won't answer him if he asks. He sees those who would participate but are either too embarrassed to answer, or are afraid they will give the wrong answer and embarrass the teacher and themselves. Further the teacher sees a rigid format of students lined up in rows, seeing only the backs of other people's heads. He also sees a group that might get upset if some conflict or disagreement should arise. So he wonders why he should take the class to teach it, or if it wouldn't be best at least to eliminate the discussion and go on with a well prepared lecture.

This isn't necessarily the way it always is, of course. Some adult classes are exciting and fruitful. The class is interested, they have studied, the teacher is acting as a catalyst only, and the group seems to be doing all the work What makes the difference? Is it the teacher? Is he just that much better than all those others who don't have classes like this one? Has he got some kind of magic formula that only a few can ever expect to have? Or maybe it's the particular group. Maybe they are just unusual. Is it really the group that makes the difference? Can one group be that much different from another one? Is it that they have just decided to study, where others just don't really care? What about the material? Is it the material that has got the group interested and working and participating? Does the material make that much difference? Is it not possible to get that kind of class going on any subject? If it is the subject matter, what subjects lend themselves to this kind of excitement? Maybe it's the environment – maybe the arrangement of the auditorium has *made* the difference? We need the answers to these questions and hopefully we will find them in this chapter.

There Are Advantages Of The Adult Class

We've already pointed out that one of the main advantages of the adult class is that there is *already* much knowledge present. Along with this is the reasoning power of the group. They can handle most any subject we're likely to get into. While some will be able to handle it better than others, either because of their background or their intellect, there will be others who will have a hard time, of course. But with all the knowledge present, there will be plenty of help for them. There is the added advantage that most of the students would rather learn than not learn. They don't want to waste their time, so would like to know that they are taking something home with them. The teacher usually has both the respect and the sympathy of the group, even though he may not realize it all the time. If he makes any effort at all not to lord it over the class, they will be very empathetic of him and the job he has.

A further advantage is that the group generally wants to avoid conflict and so will be on the teacher's side in most discussions, unless the teacher purposely or accidentally alienates them. (The teacher's attitude towards the group, the material and the assignment he's working on makes a great deal of difference on the outcome of the session being taught. If he persists in ridicule or sarcasm or in talking down to the participants, sooner or later they will "turn on him." When they do, he may be surprised and wonder why. With a little thinking he should be able to figure it out.) There is the advantage that many of the students have been over the material in the other congregations or classes they've been in before. Even if they haven't studied, they can still be of some help and contribute to the subject being discussed. Of course, one advantage is that some will have studied their lessons and will be prepared to help as the opportunity presents itself.

There Are Disadvantages

Some of the disadvantages we have already discussed. We have to admit that there are those in the class who would prefer to "hide out" and never be called on for anything. These would be offended if they were called on directly, and would not be very prepared to give the right answer anyway. And this is another disadvantage to teaching the adult class; the teacher is confronted with responsible adults who have made no effort to prepare themselves for the assignment.

They come and sit, perhaps expecting to learn something, but without putting out any effort to study, to dig into background material or even to come up with any questions for clarification. They aren't much help to the interested teacher. They are, of course, discouraging.

Another disadvantage is that there are those who have studied but don't know how they can get into the conversation. They are either too embarrassed to comment out loud or are afraid they might not be saying the right thing. So they just do the easiest thing – nothing. This is particularly true when only a few are participating.

Finally the one or two who are saying everything begin to suspect that they are "hogging" the show, so they withdraw from participation for awhile. With them gone, there is usually no one left except the one person who talks and becomes a disadvantage himself. He's the person who always has a comment, but quite often it is irrelevant or incorrect. The teacher has to decide whether to ignore it, correct it, figure it out or deal with it directly. In either of these last two cases, he probably is just reinforcing the speaker and can expect more of the same.

There is one more disadvantage we should mention. The environment of the adult class usually lends itself to poor teaching. The seats are inflexible. The group is looking straight ahead at the back of someone's head. There is the haunting dread that something will be said that will lead to controversy and the teacher will be on the spot. The teacher lacks many of the tools that make for good teaching. There is a different group every time the class assembles. There are those who were not there last week, or may be visiting for the first time. There is not the informality of the smaller classroom (if the class is conducted in the auditorium), and even the acoustics and visibility is often reduced. Something about the auditorium tends to reduce discussion rather than encourage it. The students rarely talk out loud to each other. Any conversation is in whisper form. Most of the students don't have pencils and paper, and certainly don't expect to be tested on the material, even for self-evaluation. So altogether, the whole thing makes for a bad teaching-learning environment.

But it doesn't have to be one! All of these handicaps and disadvantages can be overcome. The successful classes around the world attest to the fact that *learning can and does take place in adult classes.*

Who's At Fault?

Probably the best answer to why the adult classes are like they are is that we've spent a lifetime of training the adults to behave the way they do! While they're small children, they are involved and excited and participating because we go to great pains to see that the classes are prepared that way. We worry about not keeping them busy, about keeping their attention, about getting them to sing and move and be a vital part of the learning experience. As the students grow older, they are allowed to listen more and more and participate less and less, until finally they are adults and don't have to do anything. Those who disagree with this may say it's the other way around; the students wanted less and less to participate and the teachers let them have their way. Actually, there isn't much difference between the two. If the latter is true, then the teachers have erred in not insisting that the students be a part of the teaching-learning experience. This isn't to say that the students should have been forced to become involved against their will. What it says is that the class activities should have been such that participation was a natural part of the class. The preparation should have included plans for the students to learn by doing, by saying, by participation.

It should have been natural involvement, not strained or unreal. Had the students enjoyed the learning activities in this manner up until the time they became adults, they would not only have expected it of the teacher, but maybe insisted upon it.

Another reason the adult classes seem to be a trouble spot as far as getting participation, study and excitement is that through the years we have had many teacher training classes, but seldom or never have we had *learner* training classes. A close look at many of our teacher training classes show that even there we are discouraging participation, perhaps without knowing it. We either spend long periods studying the Bible in these classes, or have what amounts to speech training classes. Certainly it is important for the teachers to know the Bible, and Bible training classes are always urgently needed. But we should call them just what they are: Bible classes, not teacher training classes. The same is true of speech training. Everyone needs to have some kind of training in how to speak before a group, but learning to speak in front of a class isn't the secret to success in *teaching* that same class. In fact, speech training may even be self-defeating for a teacher if he or she isn't careful. One of the big problems in the adult class is that the teacher talks too much. If we give him speech training, he may gain confidence to do even more talking and provide for less class participation.

The whole point is that a good teacher training class instructs on how to get the students involved, how to get the feedback necessary to knowing how well the group is doing, and how to teach a class that consists of very much participation from as many people as possible. If we could have good teacher training classes and then extend this to the entire congregation so they would understand what it takes to learn, we would have a much better set of adult learners.

Often the preacher is the one who teaches the adult class. Now he's caught in a dilemma. He's got the background, has probably studied his lesson well and is anxious to put forth as much effort as possible to see that learning takes place. Put all this together and then put a group of adults in front of him who aren't used to getting involved and his recourse usually is to turn the class into a lecture period. On Sundays the adults get two sermons, one from the pulpit, the other from down in front. At midweek the class consists of a few people sitting up close to the front with the preacher, and the rest of the congregation scattered out towards the rear. When those in the front comment, the ones in the rear can't hear what they say. When the ones in the rear speak, the teacher has to ask them to repeat it, which discourages them from further comment. The fault, as we have said, may well lie in the training of the students to become apathetic about getting involved.

So What Are The Solutions?

First of all, let's take care of the next generation of adults coming along. Let's see that the young people who will make up the adult population in the next two or three years experience only the best in teaching and learning. Get them to expecting the enthusiastic, well prepared teacher. Let them know the advantages of learning by participating. But don't just stop here. Let's go on down to the lower ages and see that we don't break the chain of involvement in learning that starts in preschool.

In the adult classes, select teachers who are inventive enough to get the group interested and involved in the learning that's taking place. Pick teachers who know their subject, but also know good teaching techniques. ("Good teaching techniques" does not necessarily mean someone who has taught for twenty years and really knows the Bible. Experience is valuable in improving any skill, providing the practice is on the right thing, not just doing the wrong thing over and over again for twenty years.) The teacher of the adult classes should be the one who watches his audience, who knows when the group isn't "with" him. He should be one who is sensitive enough to realize when the class is getting away from him and who knows it quickly enough to do something about it before they are too far away to bring back. He's one who always has some kind of activity in the back of his mind that will successfully bring the audience to life. Not something complicated; just a simple method that gets some participation and interest, and allows the teacher to continue without too much break in his lesson plan. Again, the important thing is to have teachers *who know their audience*, and are not like many who see themselves as great teachers – not because they know that much learning is taking place, but because they know what great things they are saying.

But there is more that we can do to improve the adult class. We can be careful what we choose to study – not the topic, but the depth or length of the study. We should pick topics that can be covered in a short time (short as compared to three years in the study of one book from the Bible), remembering that in many places there is turnover in the audience from week to week, and especially from month to month. The selection of topics and how much to go into that topic should be done with a definite time frame in mind. The teacher should be able to say to the class, "We will spend three months on this and by the end of that time you will be able to..." As simple as it sounds, it facilitates learning considerably for the students to know what is expected of them and how long they have to reach that expectation. Perhaps the place this is offended the most is in "teacher training classes" where the men meet once a week to study the Bible. The class is scheduled to meet every Tuesday night and except for the summer break, there is no other time frame limitation. A better arrangement would be to specify that certain topics are going to be covered for the next six weeks, then that study will be finished. If the group wants to pick up another short-term study, then it is announced and those who are interested may come if they please, knowing that they aren't committed to continue until summer, even if the topics are of interest or help to them. The same is true for ladies' Bible classes. They should have the same kind of direction and goal. The ladies should know that if they come for a specified length of time, they will have acquired certain knowledge about certain specific things. The whole idea here is to make sure that the topics are finished, and don't just finally die a slow and sometimes painful death!

Specific Teaching Techniques

Let's look at some techniques for solving some of the "no involvement" and "no study" problems. If the class comes in and hasn't studied its lesson, the teacher isn't likely to get much meaningful discussion and participation. One alternative is for the teacher to pick up the lesson and lecture. This solves the class's problem as far as not studying is concerned, but doesn't do much for the learning situation. Another alternative is to let the group study right there in class. This doesn't mean that we insult them and accuse them of not studying. We simply assign one side of the room to "look at the first ten verses and see what one thing sticks in your mind as the key to what is being said. The other side take the last twelve verses and do the same thing. You'll have about six or seven minutes. You might talk it over with the person sitting in front of you or behind you." Such a simple operation as this does all kinds of things toward getting learning taking place. They have a purpose; they have a goal they can reach on their own; they can talk to someone else if they want to check their thoughts out; they know what is expected of them; they have a chance to check their results with others in the class when the reporting is done, they have a commitment to their opinion, they have something to talk about when class resumes, the teacher doesn't even have to be a part of the discussion if he doesn't want to be. At best, he can serve as moderator, letting the class do the thinking. Best of all, the material is being very well discussed and only those points that the group finds pertinent are being brought out for discussion. If the teacher feels they missed something, he can volunteer it. Otherwise, he lets the discussion go on until it's time to go to something else. The something else may be an exercise where the groups are now looking for a passage or word or phrase that would be confusing to someone studying this lesson for the first time. The same feedback procedures are used and the class again is much involved, with a *purpose*.

This idea of having the group look for certain things can go on endlessly if we use a little imagination. We can have the group look for possible references to the Old Testament. They can look for possible points of disagreement. They can pick out three separate ideas or the one verse that comes the closest to giving the theme of the whole chapter. The teacher can throw out a point of dispute and have the group try to find a verse that refutes the point made. One side of the class can come up with questions, the other side is challenged to answer them, then the process is reversed. Note that these are all meaningful activities, activities that will teach the specific material in the chapter or other study material being used.

Another good technique for getting the class involved is to have certain ones or groups go to the library (if the building has one) and look up something on a topic being discussed. If necessary, they can look it up between now and next class period. "See what you can find of interest to the class on the Sadducees, and tell us about it next week." Such a simple exercise as this says to the group that the teacher thinks others have something worthwhile to contribute. He is also saying they have an opportunity to be a part of the class, and it's up to them to back out. They rarely do. The important thing is to reinforce them as they contribute. In fact, few things will motivate a group much more than good reinforcement from the teacher. This isn't a *grand* and glorious bit of excitement announcing to the world that the person has contributed something worthwhile. It may be no more than a soft word of thanks, or a reference later on to something the person contributed, letting the class know that you regard the contribution as a specific part of the input to learning. "Just like Harvey said, we need to remember..." We shouldn't have to dwell on the importance of not ridiculing or embarrassing those who contribute. Not only will this not get any more from that person, but it will pretty much close the door to contribution from others as well.

Conclusion

Teaching the adults is a challenge. Sometimes it's a frustrating and seemingly hopeless task, made this way by years of training them to be just what they are as students today! Generally, we are dealing with people who already have their minds made up, so if we expect to get them to change, we'll have to do it by getting them to talk about their position, their opinion, their problems. As they talk about these things, they hear not only their own ideas for the first time (maybe) but they also see how these things affect the others. They get a chance to check their ideas out, in other words. If the teacher does all the talking, there won't be much of a test. The job of getting involvement is difficult, but not impossible.

There are techniques that give us meaningful and productive feedback and participation. The skillful teacher will practice these techniques until they are a natural part of his teaching tools. He uses them for the right purpose-to increase learning.

The *successful* teacher is always looking for ways to do just that.

DISCUSSION ACTIVITIES

1. Group discussion: Why is it that adult classes are often the ones most dreaded by teachers, especially good teachers? Is it the fault of the traditional class setup, is it the auditorium, or is it just that people want to hide in an adult class? List the findings on the board and discuss further.

2. Now look at the list and decide as a group how many of the things listed could be overcome if everyone worked at it. How many of the problems are caused by typical students- of which we are a part? Can something be done in this congregation to improve the situation, no matter how good it is already? What would it take to make these improvements?

3. Group discussion: Why is it that a group of adults can get together in a small classroom and have a fine discussion, but can't accomplish the same thing in the auditorium? Further, decide why it is that even controversial subjects can be discussed in a small class, but aren't usually acceptable in a larger group. Should something be done to break the entire group from the auditorium class into smaller groups?

4. Divide the class into two groups. One group is to be in favor of keeping classes broken into groups by ages, i.e., "young adults," "young married couples," "seniors," etc. The other group is against such an arrangement. Let them discuss this, even go into separate rooms to work on their position, then return after 20-30 minutes of discussion. Now have a debate, with each side getting two five-minute presentations. (Pro-Con-Pro-Con). After the debate, have a general discussion on the subject.

Acts 17:2

And Paul, as his manner was, went in unto them, and three sabbath days reasoned with them out of the Scriptures.

CHAPTER 13

SPECIAL CLASSES

Acts 24:24-25
And after certain days, when Felix came with his wife Drusilla, which was a Jewess, he sent for Paul, and heard him concerning the faith in Christ. And as he reasoned of righteousness, temperance, and judgment to come, Felix trembled, and answered, Go thy way for this time; when I have a convenient season, I will call for thee.

Introduction

Most congregations, at one time or another, have special classes for specific groups such as the women, young married couples, new converts, would-be speakers, etc. Often these classes are the most rewarding and productive of all the ones held by the congregations.

Even these, however, can be improved and can have some things about them that cause them to be less effective than they could be. We'll look at some important elements that make up the special classes, and see ways that we might be able to improve them.

Why Have The Class At All?

As ridiculous as it may seem, there are many times when we conduct classes without ever really deciding exactly what it is we're trying to accomplish. It may be that someone says,

"We ought to have a class for the young married couples. After all, we've got so many of them, it would make a good class." This isn't to say that it wouldn't be a good idea to have a class for the young couples, but it is to say that there ought to be a better reason for having it than just that "we've got a lot of them." Other classes fall into the same category. We have ladies' Bible classes sometimes for no better reason than that "We've always had them."

Ideally, there should be a need before we have the class. If there is, then there should also be some idea of what is going to be covered, what the group can expect to learn, how long it will take to get there, and when they can expect to finish the course.

For example, if we're going to have a young married couples' class, we should decide *ahead* of time what it is they need, either from a look at what they've studied before, from their background, or from talking to them. We should be thinking about making up a weakness in their Bible background or solving problems they might have in their newly married status. It isn't likely that we should start the class then decide that this would be a good time to study the book of Acts, 2 Samuel or Hebrews. To get the excitement needed to launch the class to keep the enthusiasm going to a successful conclusion, they should know that they are going to study a specific subject like "The Christian Home" or "Bible Couples" or "Young Men and Women in the Bible." If material isn't available, this is an excellent time to let the group do some good Bible searching. Assign different ones to come up with a family each week or report on different aspects of the Christian home. With just a little guidance, they can have a "funtime" and learn a tremendous amount at the same time.

As we have said, though, there needs to be a projected purpose and stated ending time for the study whether six weeks or six months. That way, they can keep their enthusiasm up and know that they are learning a specific thing in a specific time frame.

Training Classes?

One of the dreariest things that can happen to a good Bible teaching program is the death of a "men's training class." Many times a class will get started without any purpose and the death begins at the first meeting. Instead of being a training class, it often becomes another Bible class, where the people who come study a book of the Bible, Bible history or geography, or some study guide on the work of the church or the organization of the church. While such study is certainly good, it isn't meeting the needs of a training class. A training class should *train* someone to do something. Usually what is meant by a training class is that the men are training to be teachers. Hopefully the women aren't excluded from this training, because as talented as they are, they still need to have some guidance in how to teach. The reason these type classes often die is that there is no beginning or ending. When it starts, everyone comes out, but after awhile, the Monday-night-after-Monday-night gets to be too much. What is studied is interesting, but there is no ending place, and people begin to drop out for various reasons. Finally it just dies, or drags on with the "faithful few" hanging on, trying to build up the interest.

Those who have been successful in special classes have usually set specific objectives and specific time limits. Anyone who starts the class knows how long it will last and specifically what is to be learned. If it is a teacher-training class, then they will learn about how to teach, how to make a lesson plan, how to handle problem students and all the other things necessary to being successful as teachers. If it's a preacher training class, the men will learn how to make up outlines, how to speak well and how to use visuals. The students know why they are there and what they can learn how to do. If it's a personal work class, those attending know that they will not only know the importance of doing personal work – something we always seem to have to teach to students who apparently already know it, since they are in the class – but they will also be able to put themselves in the shoes of the person on the receiving end of personal work. Ideally, this is accomplished by role-playing, either with the class pairing off, or with the instructor being the "receiver" and anyone in the class taking him on.

The point of all this is that special classes – whether they are held on special days or Sunday or at the mid-week period- should have *definite goals and time limits*, and those attending the class should know what is expected of them and what they can expect of the class.

Teachers Should Be Chosen Carefully

The selection of teachers for a special class is a little different than the selection for the regular Bible class. They should have the same qualifications *plus* some others, usually. For example, just being a good communicator and Bible scholar isn't enough of a qualification to teach a course on evolution. An experienced person may teach a class successfully in some Bible subject, while a lack of experience is a definite handicap for someone teaching a speech training class. Bible knowledge is essential in personal work, but not enough for one teaching a personal work class. It takes some practice at role playing, and it takes experience to understand how people react when they are the recipients of personal work.

The Teacher Must Prepare Carefully And Critically

Preparation for special classes often isn't any different from any other course, but let's note a few things about the selection of material and the preparation for the course. First of all, if literature is used, be sure it really does the job. Determine the goal for the course, then select the material. Just because a book has the title "Evolution" doesn't mean it will help you reach the goal you desire in your evolution course. Examine the literature carefully, critically. Be sure that it is at the right level and directed in the right way to meet the goals you have set. Make sure it isn't too long, doesn't cover too much material, or that it isn't too short or shallow for your group of students. It isn't a bad idea to take a portion of the material in a book of study, if the book covers too much. The students can study the rest at another time or on their own, if they have developed an interest.

Often, in special classes, the best thing to do is prepare the material yourself. This way there isn't any question that it fits. There is a drawback, of course: it takes time and effort to do a good job of preparing a lesson. It may require access to some kind of duplicating equipment. Poorly prepared material is just as bad as unsuitable material that's already available. It's not impossible that the students can do much of the work themselves, however. If so, let them do it. If there is a special class to study the life of David, they all have access to the best material of all: the Bible. Let them prepare a biographical sketch of his life, making up chronological cards – with scripture references – on each event of importance in his life.

This can be done during class or before each session, taking a certain period of his life for each class period.

Seating Arrangements Should Be Flexible

Generally speaking, Most classrooms in buildings built for worship and teaching purposes are inadequate. Often the chairs or benches all face the front and can't be moved into any other arrangement because of the shape of the room. Everything we know about the furniture arrangements tells us that the worst possible situation is when the students are all facing the front, seeing only the backs of the other students' heads. There is little interchange between students because they can't see the other students and know if there is agreement or disagreement. People naturally like to see the person they're talking to, so they end up talking to the teacher when that's who they see. Ideally, the classroom should be set up in some kind of circular or semi-circular arrangement. This way all the students can see the other students, and the teacher becomes less of a dominant figure. Being at the "head" of the circle, he still can get the class to listen to him whenever he wants them to, but can also remain quiet and let them talk as long as they are in a constructive discussion.

The ideal classroom is one that allows the students to sit in the configuration that best suits the needs of that particular teaching situation. The students should be able to face each other across the room, sit in a circular arrangement or to break into small work groups without disturbing each other. We sometimes forget that most any classroom that will allow it can be arranged within a matter of seconds, if all the students pitch in to help.

Conclusion

Special classes should have a purpose. Both the teacher and the student should know what that purpose is. There should also be a time limit set on reaching these objectives. If the class decides that they want more instruction along certain lines not specified in the original goals, then another goal should be set and another time limit. The teachers should be selected with awareness to whatever special knowledge and talent is required to teach this particular subject at this particular time to this particular group of students.

The classroom should be conducive to learning, with the students seeing each other as well as the teacher. Such an arrangement will allow the students to participate more fully in the learning process.

DISCUSSION ACTIVITIES

1. Group brainstorming exercise: List all of the special classes a congregation might have over a five year period. Don't stop to discuss any of them until the list has been exhausted. Now try to arrive at a consensus of an order of importance of each of the subjects. Rank them by groups, at least, that is, the top third, middle and bottom thirds.

2. Using the list above, check off those that this congregation has had in the last five years. The list that remains is the list of special classes that might be scheduled for the next few years. Now decide who should attend these classes: men, women, both, young people, new converts, etc. Here you have a list of classes and the people who should attend. Where do you go from here?

3. From the list of special classes you've made in Question 2, that is, the list of courses that still need to be run, determine how long they should be, and whether or not they would lend themselves to weekends, concentrated sessions, Sunday afternoon sessions, week-night sessions or after Sunday or Wednesday night regular sessions. The rule here is to put the concentrated ones as those that lend themselves to learning facts or concepts, rather than practice. Song leading would obviously be done over a longer period than an overview of one book of the Bible.

4. Group brainstorming: Pick teachers from within the congregation who could teach part or all of these special classes. Draw from men or women who have professional jobs or backgrounds, such as school teachers, managers in industry; speech training, etc. Now discuss the possibility of actually scheduling some of these classes, with these people doing the teaching.

Titus 2:3-4

The aged women likewise, that they be in behaviour as becometh holiness, not false accusers, not given to much wine, teachers of good things, that they may teach the young women to be sober, to love their husbands, to love their children.

EPILOGUE

If you have made it this far, then you are to be congratulated. This is at least a strong indication that you have diligence, if nothing else. Diligence is an important ingredient in becoming a successful teacher. We hope you have learned a few things. We feel we should remind you that no one becomes an expert at teaching by the reading of a "how-to-do-it" book.

Just as in learning any skill, only practice and perhaps a few mistakes will lead to the successful performance of that skill. We think teaching is a skill that can be learned, so we hope that a few failures won't discourage you in your quest for success. Not everything we have suggested in this book will work for everyone, but all of it has worked for someone. Hopefully much of it will work for you. Finally, these admonitions:

1. Study the Bible well and often; there is no place for a Bible teacher – no matter how good – who doesn't know the subject.
2. Look to the Bible for guidance in teaching methods; inspired men taught inspired messages in inspired ways.
3. Don't ever stop trying to learn better ways of teaching; ask yourself often,

"Why am I teaching this subject this way at this time to this group?"

May the Lord bless you in your efforts!

The Authors

TOPICAL INDEX

The Authors

Sam Binkley, Jr. is a Gospel preacher with many years of preaching, both in this country and in Australia. His sermon outlines are used by many preachers, and his study books are used in Bible classes in numerous congregations. In addition to preaching, he has been successful in teaching privately and publicly, including radio and television work. Part of his teaching success has been in the area of teacher-training, and one has to sit in his Bible class only once to recognize that he practices the techniques he teaches in the teacher-training courses.

Martin M. Broadwell preached for some fifteen years while working with the Bell System as an engineer and as a training director. He travels to many parts of the world in his business, teaching teacher-training classes wherever the churches are interested. He has applied many of the principles of professional teaching to the Bible classes with much success. He is the author of a number of books on teaching and learning in the industrial world, and has prepared Bible class material using his professional experience and Bible knowledge in successful combinations.

The biographies above were included when this book was published in 1973.

31738701R00100

Made in the USA
Columbia, SC
03 November 2018